Join us on Facebook - https://www.facebook.com/groups/579682705929259

Introduction

We are a group of five people with a love of the Ninja® machines, we were drawn together firstly by a Facebook Group and secondly by a friendship formed by a mutual love of Ninja® gadgets, food and cooking. We have come together again to create a recipe book to share with you.

Our purpose this time is to cover even more range, with some classics and some vegetarian dishes, also including some sides which are our personal favourites.

The Dream Team:

Dawn Keenan Sonia Brundell Bill Kingdon Asha Joshi Amy Leggat

We come from completely different places and love to combine our own takes on dishes to bring something new and different. The team have been dedicated to testing and trying dishes to bring you flavours that will delight and inspire.

We hope you enjoy this edition.

CONTENTS

Jargon Buster

AC	AIR-CRISP (same as AIR-FRY)
AF	AIR-FRY (same as AIR-CRISP)
BROIL	GRILL (if following an American recipe)
B/R	BAKE/ROAST
FMNT	Ferment for yoghurt making on models with the yoghurt function
PC	PRESSURE COOK
PIP	Pot-in-pot
QR	QUICK RELEASE (moving from SEAL to VENT immediately after PC has completed)
NR	NATURAL RELEASE (allowing the machine to slowly release pressure after PC whilst still in SEAL mode, the keep warm light comes on and the timer starts)
NPR	Natural-pressure release (same as NR)
SAUTE	Just as you would use a pan on the hob
SC	SLOW COOK (you can use a glass lid that fits or the pressure lid on VENT. It is advisable to SAUTE on HI first to bring the pot up to heat before switching to SC)
STEAM	Have the SEAL set to VENT on the lid when using this function
STEAMBAKE	STEAM-BAKE setting
TRIVET	The holder for the AC basket on some models
TSP	Teaspoon
TBSP	Tablespoon
DSP	Dessertspoon

Model Codes

OP100	Mini Foodi 4.5L (no GRILL, dehydrate or yoghurt function)
OP300	Medium Foodi 6L (no dehydrate or yoghurt function)
OP350	Medium Foodi (same functions as Foodi Max but 6L)
OP450	Same capacity as Foodi Max (no dehydrate or yoghurt function)
OP500	Foodi Max 7.5L (has dehydrate and yoghurt function)
OL550UK	6L 11-in-1 Foodi with Smart-Lid
OL650UK	7.5L 14-in-1 Foodi with Smart-Lid
OL750UK	7.5L 15-in-1 Foodi with Smart-Lid
SP101UK	Mini flip-oven 8-in-1
DT200UK	XL Oven with 10-in-1
AG301UK	Older grill model (deeper tray)
AG551UK	Newer grill model with probe (shallow tray but more cooking surface)
AG651UK	Newest grill model with more depth for cooking and the flat Plate
AF300UK	Dual-zone Air Fryer
AF400UK	Max dual-zone Air Fryer
HB 150UK	Blender and Soup maker
JC100UK	Cold Press Juicer
ST200UK	Flip Toaster
NC300UK	Creami, sorbet, gelato and smoothie bowl maker

Useful Information

FOOD INDICATORS

The following, which is shown in the index indicates which recipes are Vegan, Vegetarian, Gluten Free and can be adapted to Gluten free by replacing the ingredients highlighted in the ingredients list. This should be useful to instantly indicate what is available.

- GF ** - Can be adapted to Gluten Free by swapping the highlighted ingredients.

- GF - Naturally Gluten free recipes do not require ingredients substitution as they are gluten free as listed

- VE – Suitable for Vegans

- V – Suitable for Vegetarians

LAYERING IDEAS

When layering a meal, anything in water is best at the very bottom in the main pot. So, these are the kind of things that would fit well:
- Rice in water
- Pasta in water
- Spaghetti in water
- Vegetables e.g., frozen vegetables in water
- New potatoes in water

For the middle layers, use the low rack sitting over the above items. To follow are some ideas of food for the centre:
- Roasted broccoli
- Small new potatoes
- Corn on the cob
- Quartered onion
- Asparagus

For the top, add the higher rack and these are the following foods that fit well:
- Chicken fillets
- Pork chops
- Steak
- Skewers

USING THE PROBE

If using the probe, insert to the centre of the meat or fish (this is the last part to cook), plug in the probe attached to the gadget and either use the pre-set temperatures or set your own. Plug the probe into the machine and you're set to go.

Select what meat you're cooking, then how rare or well done you want it to be. Chicken can only be set to well done as it can't be eaten below that temperature.

The machine will read flip when the food item needs to be turned over. If you ignore this command, it will just carry on cooking the same way up and the screen goes back to normal.

After cooking meats, leave to rest and let the juices run before serving. Wipe your probe clean, let it cool down and pack away for next time.

VENT AND SEAL – PRESSURE COOKING AND STEAMING

Both these functions need water 250ml in the main pot minimum.

When PRESSURE COOKING, the machine needs to build pressure, so the valve will need to be set to SEAL position ensuring it is closed, this is where the wobbly black valve sits in the dip, no STEAM will come out once it has reached pressure (8-15m). It takes a little while for the pressure to build and doesn't start to count down until this has completed.

Once complete it can either be set for NATURAL RELEASE or QUICK RELEASE. NATURAL RELEASE is much quieter, releasing the STEAM very slowly, when it Is fully released the machine will notify you that it is safe to open. The screen will say 'OPEN'. For QUICK RLEASE, the valve needs to move to the VENT position, lifted from the dip. It can be quite noisy, this is normal. It continues to release until all the STEAM is out and again, it will say 'OPEN', when it is completed and safe to open.

When STEAMING, the VENT valve needs to be in the VENT position, so that the STEAM can pass through the food and is release at the back VENT of the machine. Once the STEAM has built up, (8-15m) it will begin to count down the time that has been set.

There is a condensation collector at the back of some models so this will need to be emptied after any cooking using these functions.

GOOD TO KNOW

You can buy large cake cases (no more than 8") which fit in the 15/1 perfect, this is so handy when cooking greasy food, just remove and pop in the bin when finished.

Any cake tins, silicone trays or moulds that you use in your oven may be used in the Ninja® gadgets.

There are an abundance of recipe books available, but they tend to be geared towards the US market. This book is set out using UK measurements and is written in the language of a 'Ninjaholic' so is a good starting point to explore your Ninja journey.

You are encouraged to join a dedicated Facebook Group Ninja Foodi UK Recipes – Ninja Warriors which is a private Group and offers helpful posts from Group Members, recipes in files which are a great reference point and resource - together with a dose of just winging it!

When PRESSURE COOKING, always ensure the rubber SEAL is in place before putting the lid on your machine. There must always be liquid in the main pot....a quantity of 250ml is recommended as a minimum. Set the valve to SEAL position then adjust time to suit your recipe and press Start.

Before you go into an accessory buying frenzy, see what you might already have that fits your Ninja® gadget. Anything you have used in an oven before will work. Please note however, that Pyrex MUST NOT be used for PRESSURE COOKING as there is a risk it may shatter!!'

It is worth keeping foil trays from shop bought ready meals or from takeaways and recycle them in Ninja® gadgets where they may fit. These are particularly useful when making layered meals using the STEAM MEAL FUNCTION.
It is worth knowing that the lid of the Soup maker may be dismantled for ease of cleaning as the photo indicates and may be easily reassembled.

Some meals would benefit from the ability to cook two things at the same time in the basket of GRILL Models to save time and be more energy efficient. Tins to maximise the basket space are readily available as the photo below indicates.

Note: there is the risk of scratching the coating of the basket by placing metal on metal in this way.

A silicone mat placed between the main pot and cooking tin in any machine will reduce the risk of damage and scratches as well as the potential 'knocking' noise this may create and in some cases, prevent the cooking tin from 'spinning around' by the motion of the fan.

INTERESTING FACTS

Doner Kebab

The modern sandwich variant of döner kebab was derived and popularized in Berlin since the 1960s by Turkish immigrants. Nowadays there are more döner kebab stores in Berlin than in Istanbul.

Butter

Many believe that ancient nomadic people first discovered the miracle of butter. It is thought that while traveling long distances, nomads would attach sacks containing milk to their pack animals and the cream was eventually churned into butter.

Rice

The Great Wall of China is held together with sticky rice. While the Great Wall was being built during the Ming dynasty in the 15th and 16th centuries, workers used a porridge made with rice along with slaked Lime as a mortar to hold the wall's stones together.

Chicken

Did you know? It is estimated that there are more than 33 billion chickens worldwide! Outnumbering the human population

CONVERSION TABLES

WEIGHT

Imperial	Metric
½ oz	15 g
1 oz	29 g
2 oz	57 g
3 oz	85 g
4 oz	113 g
5 oz	141 g
6 oz	170 g
8 oz	227 g
10 oz	283 g
12 oz	340 g
13 oz	369 g
14 oz	397 g
15 oz	425 g
1 lb	453 g

TEMPERATURE

Fahrenheit	Celsius
100ºF	37ºC
150ºF	65ºC
200ºF	93ºC
250ºF	121ºC
300ºF	150ºC
325ºF	160ºC
350ºF	180ºC
375ºF	190ºC
400ºF	200ºC
425ºF	220ºC
450ºF	230ºC
500ºF	260ºC
525ºF	274ºC
550ºF	280ºC

ROUND CAKE TIN & LID SIZES

CM	Inches
15cm	6in
20cm	8in
23cm	9in
25cm	10in

SPOONS

Spoon size	ML
Teaspoon - tsp	5ml
Dessert Spoon - dsp	10ml
Tablespoon - tbsp	15ml

MEASUREMENTS

Cup	Ounces	Millilitres	Tablespoons
¹/16 cup	½oz	15ml	1 tbsp
⅛ cup	1oz	30ml	3 tbsp
¼ cup	2oz	59ml	4 tbsp
⅓ cup	2.5oz	79ml	5.5 tbsp
⅜ cup	3oz	90ml	6 tbsp
½ cup	4oz	118ml	8 tbsp
⅔ cup	5oz	158ml	11 tbsp
¾ cup	6oz	177ml	12 tbsp
1 cup	8oz	240ml	16 tbsp
2 cups	16oz	480ml	32 tbsp
4 cups	32oz	960ml	64 tbsp
5 cups	40oz	1180ml	80 tbsp
6 cups	48oz	1420ml	96 tbsp
8 cups	64oz	1895ml	128 tbsp

MISCELLANEOUS MEASUREMENTS

Helpful Guidance Chart – Old School Style	
1 dash	6 drops
1 pinch	1/16 tsp
1 stick of butter	¼lb/113 g
1lb sugar	2¼ cups

LITE BITES, SIDES & ACCOMPANIMENTS

PLAIN BROWN RICE

Prep Time – 3m	Cook Time – 25m	Serves – 2	Vegan✓☑	Gluten Free✓☑

Difficulty: Easy
Ninja® functions: PRESSURE COOK
Freezable: Yes, must be piping hot when reheated

INGREDIENTS

150g brown rice
350ml water
Pinch of salt
1 tsp oil

Tips/Variations: You can add a vegetable stock cube if you want a more flavoured rice.

DIRECTIONS

1. Rinse the rice until the water is clear.
2. Add the rice and water to the main pot with a pinch of salt and the oil.
3. PRESSURE COOK on HI for 9m, QUICK RELEASE.
4. Empty the water and serve.

PLAIN WHITE RICE

Prep Time – 2m	Cook Time – 3m	Serves - 2	Vegan✓⬜	Gluten Free✓⬜

Difficulty: Easy
Ninja® functions: PREESURE COOK
Freezable: Yes – make sure its piping hot
when reheated

INGREDIENTS

150g white rice
300ml of cold water
Pinch of salt

Tips/Variations: Add in a stock cube for extra flavouring.

DIRECTIONS

1. Add the rice, water and pinch of salt to the main pot.
2. PRESSURE COOK, HI heat for 3m, QUICK RELEASE.
3. Empty out the water and serve.

STUFFED PORTOBELLO MUSHROOMS

Prep Time – 5m	Cook Time – 20m	Serves – 2/4	Gluten Free✔️❓

Difficulty: Easy
Ninja® functions: AIR FRY
Freezable: No

INGREDIENTS

4 Portobello mushrooms
½ tub of garlic and herb cream cheese
¼ red onions diced very tiny
½ slice brown bread (crumbed) GF ** Use GF bread
Small handful of grated cheddar cheese

Tips/Variations: This is nice with a steak and chips. Or with a salad on the side.

GF ** - Can be adapted to Gluten Free by swapping the highlighted ingredients.

DIRECTIONS

1. Peel the mushrooms and take out the middle stem. Set aside.
2. In a bowl, mix the cream cheese, onion and half the grated cheese.
3. Spoon the mixture into each mushroom and then top with the rest of the grated cheese and finally the crumbed bread.
4. AIR FRY at 200 for 20m.

BUTTER

Prep Time – 3 to 8m	Gluten Free✓🠒

Difficulty: Easy
Ninja® functions: BLEND
Freezable: No

INGREDIENTS

600ml double cream
½ tsp salt
Water to rinse

Tips/Variations: You can add flavourings and herbs of your choice. My favourite is black pepper.

DIRECTIONS

1. Using the PROCESSOR bowl and mixing paddle (other makes can be used) add the cream to the bowl.
2. Allow the cream to come to room temperature, then select HI and mix until the solids have separated. Keep watching, it takes anything from 3 to 8m. depending on the power of your BLENDER. The 3 in 1 does it in about 4m.
3. Pour off the buttermilk, remove the butter and squeeze out using a muslin cloth.
4. Rinse the butter in a bowl of water, tip out and repeat until the water is clear. (This prolongs the life of the butter).
5. Drain and allow to stand for a minute for any remaining liquid to separate.
6. Rinse and drain once more.
7. Add the salt and pulse once or twice more to blend it in.
8. Pat to the shape of your choice and enjoy.

COMPLETE SEASONING AND SALTED CHIPS

Prep Time – 5m	Cook Time – 20m	Serves - 2	Vegetarian	Gluten Free✓

Difficulty: Easy
Ninja® functions: AIR FRY
Freezable: Yes

INGREDIENTS

2 large potatoes
1 tbsp oil
A good shake of complete seasoning GF **
Use GF Shake
Pinch of salt

Tips/Variations: You can also top with some grated cheese for cheesy, herby chips. Serve with ketchup or mayonnaise.

GF ** - Can be adapted to Gluten Free by swapping the highlighted ingredients.

DIRECTIONS

1. Peel and chip the potatoes as shown in the picture above.
2. Wash the chips well until the water runs clear.
3. Pat the chips dry using kitchen towel or a clean tea towel.
4. In a bowl, add the oil, salt and complete seasoning. Give it a good stir to coat them all in oil.
5. Cook on AIR FRY at 200 for 20m, turning halfway.

TZATZIKI

Prep Time – 5m	Cook Time – 0	Serves – 2/4	Gluten Free✓

Difficulty: Easy
Ninja® functions: 3/1 PROCESSOR grating blade
Freezable: No

INGREDIENTS

½ cucumber
2 garlic cloves minced (or 2 tsp lazy garlic®)
170g Greek yoghurt
Handful of mint leaves roughly chopped
Large pinch of salt

Tips/Variations: This can be served as a dip, with olives, pitta bread and cheese, or of course, your favourite accompaniments.

DIRECTIONS

1. Cut the cucumber in half, length ways and remove seeds with a spoon.
2. Remove the skin with a peeler. You can leave a little as it adds colour.
3. Place grating blade in 3/1 PROCESSOR and grate on slow speed until all the cucumber is grated.
4. Stir in a large pinch of salt.
5. Remove from bowl. Squeeze the cucumber to remove as much water as possible.
6. Place the cucumber into a bowl/dish and add another pinch of salt along with the remaining ingredients.
7. Stir to combine. The flavours will intensify if left to refrigerate for 1 to 2 hours before serving.

STUFFED MUSHROOM – PIZZA STYLE

Prep Time – 10m	Cook Time – 17m	Serves – Makes 6	Gluten Free✓🗆

Difficulty: Medium
Ninja® functions: AIR FRY
Freezable: No

INGREDIENTS

6 Portobello mushrooms
1 tbsp tomato paste
¼ carton of passata
Pinch of salt
¼ tsp honey
¼ tsp of thyme
¼ tsp garlic
¼ tsp oregano
1 tbsp oil
2 slices of ham (chopped)
¼ red onion (chopped)
4 pieces of chorizo (chopped)
Handful of grated cheese

Tips/Variations: You can choose your own toppings: peppers, corn and fajita chicken are also lovely toppings to have.

DIRECTIONS

1. Add the thyme, garlic and oregano to the oil and stir. After peeling the mushrooms and taking the stem out, brush with the oil mix around the bottom then turn fin side up.
2. Mix the passata, tomato paste, pinch of salt and honey together in a bowl.
3. Spread some of the tomato mix to the inner part of the mushroom.
4. Layer with chopped onion, ham and chorizo.
5. Top with the grated cheddar cheese.
6. AIR FRY in the Air Frying basket for 17m at 200.
7. Serve, with a salad as a lower carb alternative to pizza.

ROAST GARLIC AND TARTAR SAUCE

Prep Time – 5m	Serves - 2	Vegan✓⬜	Gluten Free✓⬜

Difficulty: Easy
Ninja® functions: 3/1 PROCESSOR or MINI
CHOPPER (may also be done by hand)
Freezable: No

INGREDIENTS

120g roasted garlic vegan mayonnaise
1 tsp capers (finely chopped)
90g cucumber (chopped into small chunks)
1 tsp lemon zest.

Tips/Variations: This is a quick and easy and great addition to a lovely fish dish.

DIRECTIONS

1. Place the capers and cucumber into the MINI CHOPPER and whizz down for a few seconds or until the ingredients are chopped into small pieces. (Alternatively, they may be chopped by hand).
2. Place the mayonnaise and lemon zest into a small dish and stir.
3. Add in the chopped cucumber and capers, mix together and serve.

CRAB CAKES

Prep Time – 10m	Cook Time – 120m	Serves – Makes 8

Difficulty: Medium
Ninja® functions: AIR FRY, SAUTE, BLEND
Freezable: No

INGREDIENTS

1lb crab meat
1 brown onion diced
½ red pepper
3 tbsp mayonnaise
2 eggs
1 tsp Worcester sauce
1 tsp Cajun spices
1 tsp garlic salt
½ tsp pepper
120g lightly salted crackers crumbed
(breadcrumbs can also be used)
1 tsp dried parsley (fresh can also be used)
A little oil for frying off

Tips/Variations: Perfect with the roasted garlic and tartar dip!

DIRECTIONS

1. On SAUTE MD heat, (No.3) fry off the onion and pepper in a little oil until softened. Set aside in a bowl and let it cool down.
2. Once cooled, add the mayonnaise, eggs, Worcester sauce, Cajun spices, garlic salt, pepper, parsley, whisk together then add the crab meat and salted crackers and stir together. Cover the bowl with cling film and refrigerate for 30m. (You can use a BLENDER or MINI CHOPPER to blitz down the salted crackers or breadcrumbs).
3. Remove the cling film and section into 8 equal portions, roll in your hand gently and then press down to flatten like a fish cake. AIR FRY 4 at a time on the low rack/trivet, place some foil and a little oil to stop them from sticking.
4. AIR FRY at 180 degrees for 15m, turning halfway.

ROASTED NEW POTATOES

Prep Time – 2m	Cook Time – 25m	Serves – 2/4	Vegan✓	Gluten Free✓

Difficulty: Easy
Ninja® functions: PRESSURE COOK, AIR FRY
Freezable: Yes

INGREDIENTS

1 small bag of new potatoes
Pinch of salt
2 tbsp vegetable oil

Tips/Variations: You can also add some nice herbs to this dish, just oil first, then you can add rosemary, thyme, parsley, chives to give a bit of zing.

DIRECTIONS

1. Rinse the new potatoes.
2. Fill to the 2 cups mark inside the pot with water, add in the new potatoes directly into the pot.
3. PRESSURE COOK on HI for 3m, QUICK RELEASE.
4. Empty the water.
5. Add the potatoes to a separate bowl and pour over the oil and salt.
6. Return to the air frying basket and AIR FRY at 200 degrees for around 15m, or until golden in colour.

KALE MASH

Prep Time – 10m	Cook Time – 10m	Serves – 4/6	Vegan✓	Gluten Free✓

Difficulty: Easy
Ninja® functions: PRESSURE COOK
Freezable: No

INGREDIENTS

6 medium white potatoes
1 to 2 tsp salt to taste
½ bag of chopped kale

Tips/Variations: This can be batch cooked, bagged up and frozen. Defrost and reheat on AF 200 degrees for 8m, stirring halfway.

DIRECTIONS

1. Peel and chop the potatoes into quarters.
2. Fill to the 2 cups mark inside the main pot and put the potatoes directly into the water.
3. Remove the large stems out of the kale, and roughly chop the remaining leaves.
4. Place the chopped kale leaves on top of the potatoes.
5. PRESSURE COOK on HI for 4m, QUICK RELEASE.
6. Drain the water but set aside.
7. Mash the potatoes, adding a little of your reserved water back in until it is smooth and to the desired consistency, add salt to taste before serving.

CHEESE TOPPED CHEESE, RED ONION AND PEPPER SANDWICH

Prep Time – 10m	Cook Time – 6m	Serves – 1	Gluten Free✓

Difficulty: Easy
Ninja® functions: AIR FRY
Freezable: No

INGREDIENTS

2 slices of bread GF ** Use GF bread
Butter to spread
¼ red onion sliced
½ tsp Dijon mustard
1 heaped tsp mayonnaise
Handful of grated cheddar cheese
1 Sliced small bell pepper
Parsley to top
Black pepper

Tips/Variations: You can also add ham, chorizo, onion, peperoni and peppers. Make it your own with the flavours you love.

GF ** - Can be adapted to Gluten Free by swapping the highlighted ingredients.

DIRECTIONS

1. Butter the bread, spread on the Dijon mustard, then spread on the mayonnaise.
2. Add a layer of cheese, followed by the sliced onion and a little bell pepper.
3. Add the second slice of bread and top with more grated cheese with a couple of slices of bell pepper for decoration and a sprinkle of black pepper and parsley.
4. On AIR FRY, cook the sandwich for 6 to 7m at 200 degrees or until it's all bubbling and the cheese has melted. Enjoy.

ROASTED BEEF STOCK, SAGE AND SALT POTATOES

Prep Time – 10m	Cook Time – 35m	Serves – 4	Gluten Free✓

Difficulty: Easy
Ninja® functions: PRESSURE COOK, AIR FRY
Freezable: Yes

INGREDIENTS

4 medium potatoes
2 beef stock cubes GF ** Use GF cubes
1 tbsp dried sage
Salt to taste.
1 tbsp oil

Tips/Variations: Also nice with chicken flavour

GF ** - Can be adapted to Gluten Free by
swapping the highlighted ingredients.

DIRECTIONS

1. Peel and chop the potatoes into 4.
2. Fill the main pot up to 2 cups mark with water.
3. PRESSURE COOK on HI for 3m, QUICK RELEASE. Empty out the water and put the potatoes into a bowl.
4. Sprinkle on the stock cube, salt, oil and sage and give it a gentle stir so the potatoes are coated.
5. Add to the air frying basket and AIR FRY for 25m at 180 degrees. Turn halfway.
6. Serve.

SMOOTH PEANUT BUTTER

Prep Time – 5m	Serves – Small jar	Vegan✓🟦	Gluten Free✓🟦

Difficulty: Easy
Ninja® functions: 3/1 PROCESSOR, CHOP, PUREE, MIX
Freezable: No

INGREDIENTS

400g roasted, salted peanuts
1 tsp olive oil

Tips/Variations: You can leave it chunky if you're wanting a chunkier Peanut butter.

GF** check contents for 'May Contain' to make sure its gluten free

DIRECTIONS

1. Place the peanuts into the small food PROCESSOR bowl.
2. Use the CHOP setting 3 times or until the peanuts are chopped to your liking.
3. Select the PUREE setting, do this 4 times. Scrape down the sides a little.
4. Check the consistency, if you want to loosen it up a little, pour in a teaspoon of oil, then PUREE twice more.
5. To finish up, put on the MIX setting once.

CHEESE, CHORIZO, HAM AND RED ONION PITTA POCKET

Prep Time – 2m	Cook Time – 8m	Serves – 1	Gluten Free✓

Difficulty: Easy
Ninja® functions: PANINI PRESS
Freezable: No

INGREDIENTS

2 slices of Ham (wafer thin)
2 slices of chorizo
2 slices of red onion
2 slices of cheese (pre-sliced) or cut your own.
1 tsp Dijon mustard
1 tbsp mayonnaise
1 pitta pocket GF ** Use GF pitta breads
Margarine for spreading

Tips/Variations: Also nice with bacon or pepperoni.

GF ** - Can be adapted to Gluten Free by swapping the highlighted ingredients.

DIRECTIONS

1. Spread the margarine in the inside of the pitta pocket.
2. Add a spreading of mustard, followed by the mayonnaise.
3. Layer in the cheese, chorizo, ham and red onion.
4. Place in the PANINI PRESS and cook for 8m, at 205 degrees.
5. Enjoy!

GRILLED MOZZARELLA AND MUSHROOM SANDWICH

Prep Time – 5m	Cook Time – 10/12m	Serves – 1	Gluten Free✓▢

Difficulty: Easy/Medium
Ninja® functions: BAGEL SETTING, GRILL
Freezable: No

INGREDIENTS

2 slices of mozzarella, 2cm thick slices
1 brioche bun sliced GF ** Use GF Bun
Small handful of mushrooms, sliced
Small handful of lettuce leaves, chopped
1 tomato sliced
A few slices of cucumber
Pinch of salt
Large pinch of pepper
1 tbsp butter

Tips/Variations: You can also add chopped up bacon or ham for a meatier version.

GF ** - Can be adapted to Gluten Free by swapping the highlighted ingredients.

DIRECTIONS

1. Toast the top of the bun on BAGEL SETTING 3 and set aside.
2. In a small ovenproof dish/tin or ramekin, add the sliced mushrooms with the butter, salt and pepper, giving them a stir to coat with the butter and seasoning.
3. Place the tomato slices at the bottom of the bun and top with the mozzarella.
4. Place the mushrooms and loaded bun base side by side on to the grill plate, set to GRILL, HI heat for 7m, checking the mushrooms to ensure they are cooked. Once the mozzarella is cooked but not fully melted, remove the bun base from the gill.
5. Lift the mozzarella up a little and insert the lettuce and cucumber slices, top with the mushrooms and add the bun lid. Serve.

YORKSHIRE IN THE 3/1 TOASTER

Prep Time – 5m	Cook Time – 23m	Serves – 1 large or 2 halves

Difficulty: Easy/Medium
Ninja® functions: BAKE
Freezable: Yes

INGREDIENTS

35g plain flour
35g milk
1 egg
Pinch of salt
½ tbsp oil

Tips/Variations: Serve with roast meats, vegetables and lashings of gravy.

DIRECTIONS

1. Mix the milk, flour, egg and salt. Using a hand whisk or blender to create a batter and set aside.
2. Add the oil to an ovenproof tin/dish, 6" or longer, as it rose very high, you may need a little splash more of oil if yours is longer.
3. In the tray, with the panini press removed, heat the oil in the dish on the BAKE, HI heat (205) for 10m, so it is piping hot. Carefully pour in the batter into the heated oil.
4. BAKE on HI heat (205 degrees) for around 23m.
5. Try not to check the cooking progress until the very end of cooking as otherwise, it may sink immediately.
6. This makes one large portion, or you can half and share it for two smaller portions.

NAAN BREAD CHEESE AND CHORIZO PIZZA

Prep Time – 10m	Cook Time – 4m	Serves – 1	Gluten Free✓⊡

Difficulty: Easy
Ninja® functions: PANINI SETTING
Freezable: No

INGREDIENTS

1 medium sized naan bread GF ** Use GF naan bread
1 tbsp tomato puree
1 tbsp tomato ketchup
1 tsp honey
1 tsp oregano
Handful of grated mature cheddar
4 chorizo slices chopped
Sweet chilli dip to serve - optional

Tips/Variations: You can add any variation of toppings you like. Mushrooms, peppers, precooked bacon, onion, sweetcorn.

GF ** - Can be adapted to Gluten Free by swapping the highlighted ingredients.

DIRECTIONS

1. Mix the tomato puree, ketchup, honey and oregano together and spread over the naan bread.
2. Top with the chorizo slices.
3. Add the grated cheese.
4. Place in the main toaster tray with the panini press removed.
5. Cook on PANINI SETTING for 4m on 205 degrees, HI heat.
6. Enjoy with some sweet chilli dip.

VEGETABLE TRAY BAKE FOR ONE

Prep Time – 5m	Cook Time – 20m	Serves – 1	Vegan✓	Gluten Free✓

Difficulty: Easy
Ninja® functions: BAKE
Freezable: No

INGREDIENTS

½ can of sweetcorn
3 to 4 florets of broccoli
½ red onion chopped
Handful peppers chopped
¼ tsp chilli
¼ tsp salt
¼ tsp garlic powder
½ tsp onion powder
¼ tsp black pepper
½ tsp dried oregano
1 tsp cumin
1 tbsp oil

Tips/Variations: Other vegetables such as peas, small broccoli pieces, mushrooms etc will also work well.

DIRECTIONS

1. Add all the above ingredients to a bowl and stir to combine and coat all the vegetables with the spices and oil.
2. Add to the main tray of your machine, (I used the toaster, but it can be done in any of the machines with the BAKE function).
3. Cook on BAKE setting at 200 degrees for 20m, turning halfway.
4. Serve on a bed of salad leaves.

GARLIC, HERB AND CRISPY BACON POTATO SALAD

Prep Time – 5m	Cook Time – 20m	Serves – 2	Gluten Free✓

Difficulty: Easy, Medium
Ninja® functions: PRESSURE COOK, AIR FRY
Freezable: No

INGREDIENTS

2 medium potatoes, quartered
2 bacon rashers, smoked
½ tsp oregano
¼ tsp salt
1 tsp chives
1 garlic clove crushed
¼ tsp black pepper
1 tsp honey
Lemon wedge – (Juice only)
½ tub cream cheese
2 tbsp natural yoghurt

Tips/Variations: This works well with new potatoes, skins on!

DIRECTIONS

1. Fill the pot with water to the 2 cups mark, add the chopped potatoes to it and PRESSURE COOK on HI for 3m, QUICK RELEASE. Drain the water and set aside to cool down.
2. AIR FRY your bacon rashers at 200 degrees for 8m, turning halfway. Once cooled, chop up into small pieces.
3. Add the chives, garlic, black pepper, lemon juice, cream cheese, salt, honey and yoghurt to a dish and mix it all together to combine.
4. Add to the potatoes with the chopped bacon rashers and stir gently to coat them all.
5. Top with oregano to serve.

NINJA® MASH IN A FLASH

Prep Time – 15m	Cook Time – 17m	Serves – One Complete Recipe	Gluten Free✓🔲

Difficulty: Easy
Ninja® functions: PRESSURE COOK
Freezable: Yes

INGREDIENTS

1 kg potatoes peeled (Maris Pipers
recommended)
250ml cold water
1 raw egg

Tips/Variations: You can also use milk instead of the egg if you prefer, or butter, or both. This can be batch cooked and frozen into portions as required.

DIRECTIONS

1. Add 250 ml of cold water to the main pot.
2. Chop the peeled potatoes into chunks (approx. 5cm pieces) Add to the air frying basket and place it into the main pot.
3. Make sure the valve is set to the SEAL position, then select the PRESSURE COOK function and set it for 6m.
4. If using the 15/1 select DELAYED RELEASE and set for 1m. If not, leave for 1m to NATURAL RELEASE followed by QUICK RELEASE.
5. When PRESSURE COOK cycle is complete, remove the air frying basket from the main pot and drain the water.
6. If using a metal masher or potato ricer tool, transfer the potatoes to a different pan or bowl.
7. Crack one raw egg into the PRESSURE COOKED potatoes and mash together until lumps have disappeared and a creamy texture is achieved.

GOOEY BAKED CAMEMBERT AND PETIT PAINS

Prep Time – 5m	Cook Time – 20m	Serves – 2

Difficulty: Easy
Ninja® functions: BAKE, AIR FRY
Freezable: No

INGREDIENTS

1 baking Camembert disc
1 pack part baked petit pains
Cold water

**Tips/Variations: Some Camembert discs come with either a ceramic, or wooden dish. Both of which may be used in your machine. If it doesn't then any ovenproof dish that fits your machine may be used.
Perfect with a large glass of Merlot!**

DIRECTIONS

1. Remove the Camembert disc from the fridge ½ an hour before cooking.
2. Cut a 'cross' incision in the centre of the Camembert disc, place it into the air frying basket of your machine and select the BAKE function set to 160 degrees for 15 mins and press START.
3. Lightly dampen the petit pains with cold water and place in the air frying basket next to the Camembert. Using a fork or tongs, peel back the rind of the Camembert.
4. Select the AIR FRY function and set to 170 degrees for 4 mins and continue to cook the Camembert with the petit pains.

'CHEATSWAY' GARLIC BREAD

Prep Time – 5m	Cook Time – 6m	Serves – 4

Difficulty: Easy
Ninja® functions: BAKE, AIR FRY
Freezable: No

INGREDIENTS

1 pack of part baked rolls
50g salted butter
2 tsp garlic granules
Grated Cheese
Fresh or dried chives (for garnish)

Tips/Variations: Can also be cooked from frozen. Just add a few more mins cooking time and be careful with the knife when slicing frozen rolls.
Great as a starter to jazz up a mid-week meal.

DIRECTIONS

1. Mix the butter and garlic granules together to create the garlic butter.
2. Lightly dampen the rolls with cold water.
3. Slice rolls in half and spread with the garlic butter.
4. Place the air frying basket into the machine, arrange the sliced rolls into it and select the BAKE function set at 180 degrees and cook for 3 mins.
5. Top the sliced rolls with grated cheese and chives and switch the machine to AIR FRY function set at 180 degrees and cook for a further 3 mins or until the cheese is browned and bubbly to personal liking.

PANEER TIKKA WRAP

Prep Time – 5m	Cook Time – 15m	Serves – 2 to 4

Difficulty: Easy
Ninja® functions: AIR FRY
Freezable: No

INGREDIENTS

1 slab of shop bought Paneer (cut into 2cm chunks)
1 – 2 tsp Shan® tikka seasoning
½ a small lemon (juice only)
4 small tortilla wraps
Fresh finger chilli finely chopped (optional)
Finely chopped coriander (for garnish)
Yoghurt and mint sauce (see Tips / Variations)
Chopped salad (of choice)

Tips/Variations: Paneer is a versatile hard Indian cheese readily available in most large Supermarkets or from Asian Grocery Stores. Homemade mint sauce may be created using 2 tbsp of natural low-fat yoghurt with one teaspoon of mint sauce and stirred together. The paneer chunks could also be threaded onto skewers with sliced vegetables to create a meat free style kebab.

DIRECTIONS

1. Place the Paneer chunks into a lidded container and sprinkle on the tikka Seasoning. Close the lid and give the container a shake to evenly coat with the seasoning.
2. Select the AIR FRY function on the machine and set to 180 degrees and cook the Paneer for 9 mins with periodic moving around.
3. Add in the wraps and continue to cook for a further 1 min. Remove the wraps from the machine and squeeze the lemon juice onto the Paneer.
4. Assemble the paneer into the wraps with salad and homemade mint sauce.

POTATO AND PEA SAMOSAS

Prep Time – 30m	Cook Time – 1hr	Serves – 12

Difficulty: Medium
Ninja® functions: SAUTE, AIR FRY
Freezable: Yes

INGREDIENTS

4 medium white potatoes (finely diced)
2 medium onions (peeled and finely diced)
2 green finger chillies (chopped)
1 cup of frozen peas
A handful of fresh coriander (coarsely chopped)
3 tsp Shan® vegetable masala
2 tsp mustard seeds
2 tsp cumin seeds
1 tbsp cooking oil
1 pack filo pastry sheets
Spray oil (rapeseed recommended)

Tips/Variations: These may be cooled and frozen and can be reheated from frozen using the AIR FRY function.

DIRECTIONS

1. Select the SEAR/SAUTE function and set to HI (No. 5) and add the oil.
2. Once the oil has heated through, add in the onions, potatoes, cumin seeds and mustard seeds. Reduce heat to MD (No. 4) and SAUTE the mixture until the onions have softened with a periodic stir. Note: during this step, you may need to switch between heat settings HI (No. 5) and MD (No. 4) to ensure the potatoes are cooked through and this will also depend on the 'chopped' size of them.
3. Add in the vegetable masala, chopped chillies, frozen peas and continue to SAUTE on MD heat (No. 4) until the potatoes are cooked and the peas have defrosted and heated through.
4. Mix in the chopped coriander and leave to one side to cool.
5. Refer to any online video on how to fold the perfect samosa triangle and follow this method to bring together the filo pastry sheets with the prepared samosa filling to create the samosa triangles.
6. Lightly spray each samosa with rapeseed oil. You can use a pastry brush to ensure an even coverage.
7. Select the AIR FRY function on your machine and with the air frying basket in place pre-heat the machine on 170 degrees for 3 mins.
8. Arrange the samosas into the air frying basket and cook for 3 mins each side until they are golden and crispy. Adjust cooking time if required.

SPICY COCKTAIL SCOTCH EGGS

Prep Time – 15m	Cook Time – 20m	Serves – One complete recipe	Gluten Free✓⏾

Difficulty: Easy
Ninja® functions: STEAM, AIR FRY
Freezable: No

INGREDIENTS

12 quail eggs
250ml cold water
Cold water with ice (enough to submerge the cooked eggs into)
1 pack sausage meat (500g) GF ** Use GF sausage meat
2-3 small red chillies (finely chopped and adjusted to personal heat preference)
A handful of fresh coriander (leaves only, finely chopped)
1 ½ tsp ground cumin
1 pack of shop bought golden breadcrumbs GF ** Use GF breadcrumbs

Tips/Variations: If hand mixing the sausage meat, it is advisable to use plastic gloves to avoid contact of chilli to eyes. It is also advisable to use gloves when forming balls of the eggs and the sausage meat.
A glass lid that fits the machine may be used instead of the SMART LID on your machine.

GF ** - Can be adapted to Gluten Free by swapping the highlighted ingredients.

DIRECTIONS

1. Pour the 250ml cold water into the main pot. Place the low rack into the pot and arrange the quail eggs onto it. Close the SMARTLID and ensure the valve is set to VENT. Select the STEAM function and set the time to 1 min and press START.
2. In the meantime, prepare a container with cold water and ice.
3. When the STEAM cycle completes, remove the eggs immediately from the machine and plunge into the iced water. Once the eggs are cool enough, peel them and set aside.
4. Combine the sausage meat, chillies, coriander and ground cumin together (this can be done either by hand or blitzed together in a blender).
5. Divide the sausage mixture evenly into 12 portions. Roll each portion into a ball, then flatten out to form a thin patty. Wrap each patty around the peeled eggs, smoothing out the join and ensuring there is no egg left exposed.
6. Sprinkle the golden breadcrumbs into a clean work surface and then roll each of the scotch eggs in the crumbs to coat all over.
7. Arrange the scotch eggs in the air frying basket of the machine. Note: depending on size, the scotch eggs may need to be cooked in two batches.
8. Select the AIR FRY function and set to 180 degrees for 10 mins and cook the scotch eggs through, with periodic turning. Adjust cooking time if required.

PUB CLASSICS & FAKEAWAYS

CHICKEN, HAM AND MUSHROOM PASTRY

Prep Time – 15m	Cook Time – 25m	Serves – 6

Difficulty: Easy/Medium
Ninja® functions: SAUTE, AIR FRY
Freezable: Yes, must be re-heated properly

INGREDIENTS

4 chicken breasts diced small
4 slices of thick ham diced
8 sliced mushrooms
2 packs Ready Roll puff pastry (room temperature)
400ml milk
4 chicken stock cubes
1 tbsp plain flour
½ tsp salt
1 tsp dried parsley
½ tsp dried sage
A little milk or a whisked egg to brush the pastry
2 tbsp oil

Tips/Variations: The ingredients can be changed, for example, gammon, onions and leeks are a good combination.

DIRECTIONS

1. Add the oil and diced chicken to the pot on SAUTE, MD heat (No. 3) until the chicken has cooked. Then add the ham and mushrooms, keep stirring periodically until it is all cooked.
2. Add the flour and stir to coat the mixture, followed by the milk, stock cubes, salt, sage and parsley. Continue to stir through, it should thicken and continue to cook whilst it is simmering and then switch off.
3. Slice the pastry sheet into 6 equal parts, do this with both packs, so you have a bottom and a top for 6 pastries. (I cut the parchment paper they come on into 6 too, it's easier to lift in and out of the machine).
4. Spoon the mixture onto 6 bases, leaving space around the edge. Add the top pastry sheet.
5. Using a fork, press the two pastry layers together around the edges to seal the pastry and cut a little slit in the top to allow the heat to escape.
6. Brush the top with milk or whisked egg and cook on AIR FRY at 200 degrees, for around 10 to 15m

BBQ PULLED CHICKEN

Prep Time – 10m	Cook Time – 25m	Serves - 2

Difficulty: Medium
Ninja® functions: ROAST/BAKE
Freezable: No

INGREDIENTS

2 chicken breasts
1 tbsp hoisin sauce
1 ½ tsp whole grain mustard
1 dsp tomato puree
1 tbsp mayonnaise
1 tbsp Worcester sauce
1 tsp cider vinegar
2 brioche burger buns
1 dsp tomato ketchup
1 chicken stock cubes
1 tbsp sugar
50m hot water

Tips/Variations: This is great served with wedges and a side salad.
If using the dual, the other drawer may be used to make the fries.
If using the multicooker, the wedges may be cooked under the rack whilst the chicken is being cooked.

DIRECTIONS

1. Dissolve the stock cubes into 50ml of hot water, mix in the tomato puree, ketchup, hoisin sauce, mustard, Worcester sauce, sugar and a pinch of black pepper.
2. Place the chicken in an oven proof dish (takeaway foil containers are perfect for this, as well as a silicone mould or even a cake tin).
3. Pour all the sauce over the chicken.
4. Set to ROAST/BAKE function at 180 degrees, place on lower rack and cook for 20/25m. You can place on low rack in the dual also.
5. To make the zingy mayonnaise sauce, mix the mayonnaise and cider vinegar together.
6. Remove the chicken to a chopping board and shred with two forks, then return the chicken to the sauce mix. In the meantime, the cut buns can be warming in the machine.
7. Build the burger, by filling the base with the chicken sauce, topped with zingy mayonnaise and place the chicken on the top followed by the bun lid.

KAY FC TOWER BURGER

Prep Time – 10m	Cook Time – 20m	Serves - 2

Difficulty: Medium
Ninja® functions: AIR FRY, MINI CHOPPER (if you have one)
Freezable: No

INGREDIENTS

2 chicken breasts
2 tsp each of salt, onion powder and garlic powder
1 tsp black pepper
1 tsp white pepper
2 tsp dried mustard
½ tsp each of paprika, oregano, thyme, basil
2 tsp ground ginger
5 tbsp flour
1 cup buttermilk
5 tbsp oil
2 bread rolls
2 slices of lettuce
2 hash browns
2 cheese square's
1 tbsp each of mayonnaise and ketchup

Tips/Variations: This is perfect served with fries and some baked beans with a dash of BBQ sauce mixed in. Just like the real thing.

DIRECTIONS

1. Add the flour, salt, onion powder, garlic powder, black pepper, white pepper, dried mustard, paprika, oregano, thyme, basil and ground ginger into a bowl and mix. Set aside
2. Pour the butter milk into a bowl and dip the chicken breasts into it turning to coat both sides. Shake off any excess, then place the chicken into the flour/spice mix, making sure it is completely covered on both sides.
3. In the main pot, add the oil and shallow fry both sides of the chicken on SAUTE, HI heat (No.5) for 2m each side. Remove and clean pot.
4. Now, in the air fry basket AIR FRY for 20m at 200 degrees, turning halfway (or use your probe) Add the hash browns in when there is 10m left to finish off together.
5. Build the tower as follows – On the bread roll base, add a squeeze of mayonnaise, lettuce, the breaded chicken, cheese square, ketchup and the hash brown, top with the burger bun lid and enjoy!

BIG MACK

Prep Time – 5 to 10m	Cook Time – 8m	Serves - 4

Difficulty: Easy/Medium
Ninja® functions: BLENDER, GRILL
Freezable: Yes

INGREDIENTS

500g lean minced beef
1 tbsp English mustard
2 tsp salt
2 beef stock cubes
1 tsp pepper
½ onion diced tiny
Fresh lettuce leaves
Sliced pickled gherkins, a couple for each
8 burger cheese squares
6 burger Buns
For the burger sauce:
2 tbsp mayonnaise
1 tbsp ketchup
½ tbsp mustard
1 tsp pickle juice from the pickled gherkins

Tips/Variations: Serve with fries and a coke!

DIRECTIONS

1. Add the beef, mustard, salt, crumbled stock cubes and pepper to the BLENDER and whizz until it's all mixed in. I did this for around 1 to 2m stopping and pushing it all down once.
2. Take out the mixture and make one big ball, push it down, now cut into 8 pieces.
3. If you have a burger press, use that to make 8 burgers. If not, roll each one into a ball, then press down to make it flat, I use a spatula to make it flat and thin. Add to parchment paper.
4. GRILL, HI heat for around 8 to 10m, turning halfway until cooked on each side. Add the cheese 1m before the end to melt on top. Add all the ingredients together for the burger sauce.
5. Now you are going to need 4 burger buns and the bottoms from the extra 2, to make the middle part of the big mack bun, (I can get two from one bun by cutting the very top off, then slicing the rest into two halves).
6. To assemble your big mack, add some burger sauce to the bun, next add a sprinkle of the diced onion, lettuce, a beef patty with the melted cheese and pickle slices. Then add the next middle bun piece and repeat the process again. Then finally the top bun. Enjoy!

POSH LOADED FRIES

Prep Time – 20m	Cook Time – 50m	Serves - 4	Gluten free✓🆓

Difficulty: Medium
Ninja® functions: SAUTE, AIR FRY
Freezable: Yes

INGREDIENTS

Fries:
3 large potatoes
1 tbsp oil
Loaded Beef:
500g lean minced beef
1 can of chopped toms – refill with water
1 brown onion diced
1 pack of taco seasoning mix GF ** Use GF
2 beef stock cubes GF ** Use GF stock cubes
1 small glass of red wine
1 tsp Lazy Garlic®
3 x streaky bacon, unsmoked, chopped
3 tbsp tomato paste
1 tbsp honey
1 carton passata
Handful of red Leicester cheese
Crème fraiche and dried chives to top

Tips/Variations: Also nice with cheddar cheese and the beef mix can be served on a bed of nachos, I also added a little sriracha sauce for some heat

GF ** - Can be adapted to Gluten Free by swapping the highlighted ingredients.

DIRECTIONS

1. Peel and chip the potatoes, then wash, pat dry, oil and salt. AIR FRY for 20m 200 degrees. Set aside.
2. Add the beef, onion, garlic and bacon to the main pot and SAUTE MD heat (No.3). Once browned off add the tomatoes, water, taco mix, stock cubes, wine, tomato paste, honey, passata and salt to taste. Stir and leave for several minutes for the ingredients to heat through. You may need to reduce heat to LO/MD (No.2).
3. Empty the pot.
4. In an ovenproof dish, or the main pot (I used the grill), add the chips to the bottom, AIR FRY at 200 degrees for 5m to bring back to heat, then add the beef to the top, with the cheese over it, AIR FRY for a further 8m or until it is hot and the cheese is melted.
5. Top with sour cream or crème fraiche and chives to serve.

DOUBLE SAUSAGE AND EGG MUFFIN

Prep Time – 5m	Cook Time – 20m	Serves - 2	Gluten free✓☐

Difficulty: Easy
Ninja® functions: AIR FRY, STEAM
Freezable: No

INGREDIENTS

4 to 6 good quality sausages, skinned GF **
use GF sausage meat
4 white muffin Rolls GF ** Use GF muffins
2 burger cheese slices
2 eggs (I used small in silicone egg moulds)

Tips/Variations: Serve with a hash brown and ketchup, flip top head required!

GF ** - Can be adapted to Gluten Free by swapping the highlighted ingredients.

DIRECTIONS

1. Squeeze out the sausage meat from the skins and roll into a ball, flatten down into thin patties, you may want to make them bigger by doing 1.5 sausages for each burger.
2. AIR FRY for around 8m at 210 degrees, turning halfway, set aside.
3. Spray the silicone egg moulds with oil and rub around to coat them.
4. Add the eggs to the moulds (mine were straight out of the fridge).
5. Fill the main pot with water to the 2 cups mark.
6. Add the mould directly to the water to the side of the pot to stop them falling over.
7. STEAM for 2 to 3m, vent open, check if they need a little longer if your eggs are larger.
8. Remove as soon as they're cooked, keeping them in the moulds, cover with a little foil to keep warm, empty the water.
9. Add the burgers to the air fry basket and cook for 2m on GRILL HI heat, adding the buns for the last minute.
10. Layer the Muffin – Bottom half of the muffin, then a sausage burger, then cheese, then burger, then lastly your egg. (I used a dessert spoon to get it out easy) Crown with the muffin top and enjoy!

BEEF, BACON AND MUSHROOM PIE WITH CHIPS

Prep Time – 15m	Cook Time – 50m	Serves - 4

Difficulty: Easy
Ninja® functions: SAUTE, PRESSURE COOK, AIR FRY
Freezable: Yes

INGREDIENTS

500g diced beef
1 pack of shortcrust pastry
1 pack of puff pastry
1 large, diced onion
Large handful of diced mushrooms
4 strips of bacon diced (unsmoked)
2 tbsp plain flour
4 x beef stock cubes
1 tsp sage
1 tsp parsley
700ml water boiled
Salt to taste + 1 tbsp oil + egg to brush pastry
For the chips:
4 medium potatoes peeled and chipped.
Salt to taste + oil to coat chips

Tips/Variations: If using a small machine, you can set aside the chips, whilst doing the pies, then add back in for 3/4m at the end.

DIRECTIONS

1. In the main pot on SAUTE, MD heat (No. 3) add the oil, onions, bacon and mushrooms. Cook through. Add the beef and cook until browned, turn down to LO/MD heat (No. 2)
2. Add the stock cubes and the plain flour, stir around to coat the food, then add in the hot water, stirring whilst adding. The gravy should thicken. Add the sage, parsley and salt to taste. PRESSURE COOK, on HI heat for 5m, QUICK RELEASE. Thicken with cornflour if needed. Set aside
3. Wash the peeled and chipped potatoes, pat dry, add to a bowl, stir in the salt and oil. AIR FRY for 20m at 200 degrees. Shake halfway.
4. Whilst the chips are cooking, lay out the shortcrust pastry, cut into 4, roll out a little more if you need to make it bigger, then add to the dish that the pie is going in. Grease it first. Blind BAKE for 8m at 190 degrees. (Baking beads, can be used to stop it raising). Remove.
5. Add the filling, then cut the puff pastry into 4 and add to the top, cutting off any overhang. Crimp together with a fork. Brush the top with milk or whisked egg. Add a slit to the top for the steam to come out. Cook for 12m on AIR FRY at 190 degrees and serve with the chips.

CHICKEN HOT POT

Prep Time – 15m	Cook Time – 2 hrs 10m	Serves - 4	Gluten free✓⌷

Difficulty: Easy/Medium
Ninja® functions: SAUTE, BAKE
Freezable: No

INGREDIENTS

4 chicken breasts diced
800g potatoes peeled and sliced
1 onion diced
1 carrot diced
100g turnip diced
½ cup frozen peas
2 chicken stock cubes in a pint of hot water GF
** Use GF stock cubes
1 tsp dried sage
1 tsp dried rosemary
1 tsp dried thyme
Salt and pepper to taste
2 tbsp plain flour GF ** Use GF flour
2 tbsp oil

Equipment required
2 x 7" deep tin for the Foodi and dual
12 inch to fit the 10/1

Tips/Variations: Lovely with a nice glass of white wine.

GF ** - Can be adapted to Gluten Free by swapping the highlighted ingredients.

DIRECTIONS

1. In a jug, add the crumbled stock cubes and pour in the hot water to dissolve.
2. On SAUTE, HI heat (No. 5) add the oil to heat, turn down to MD (No.3). Salt and pepper the diced chicken, then add to the oil to brown off.
3. Add the onion to the oil to soften, when ready, add the flour and stir together, add the thyme, sage and rosemary and stir to coat the onions. Turn off.
4. Lay the potatoes in the tin, then the chicken, onions, carrots, peas and turnip. Then another layer of the same thing, finish with a layer of potatoes.
5. Pour the stock over it all and double cover with foil, securing tight
6. On the BAKE function, cook for 2 hours at 200 degrees. Remove foil. Spread the potatoes with butter and BAKE at 200 degrees for 5 to 10m more to brown the top. Serve.

BEEF IN STOUT

Prep Time – 20m	Cook Time – 4hrs	Serves – 4

Difficulty: Easy
Ninja® functions: SEAR/SAUTE, SLOW COOK
Freezable: Yes

INGREDIENTS

1 tbsp olive oil
4 echalion shallots (peeled and coarsely chopped)
800g diced beef
30g plain flour
1 tsp ground black pepper
1 heaped tbsp tomato puree
400ml stout
300ml beef stock
3 sprigs fresh rosemary (leaves only)
3 large carrots (peeled and cut in 3cm batons)
4 parsnips (peeled and cut in pieces 3cm batons)

**Tips/Variations: This goes perfectly with mashed potatoes which can be made beforehand.
For a thicker gravy, stir in some thickening granules at the time of adding in the vegetables. Onion may be used instead of shallots.
Note: On some machines the Slow Cook default time is 4 hours, so set an alarm for 2 hours.
In the event of leftovers, a puff pastry top may be added to create a pie or frozen for another meal!**

DIRECTIONS

1. Place the beef, flour and pepper in a large mixing bowl and mix together until the meat is coated in the flour and leave to one side.
2. Select the SEAR/SAUTE function and set to HI (No. 5). Add in the olive oil to heat through and add in the onions. Stir for a few mins to release the onion aroma.
3. Add in the seasoned beef and stir until the meat is sealed all over.
4. Reduce heat to MD (No. 3) and add in the tomato puree, stout, rosemary and stock. Stir everything together until it is bubbling.
5. Switch to SLOW COOK function, HI heat, place lid set to VENT, (Alternatively you can use a glass lid that fits over the main pot) and leave for 2 hours.
6. Add in the carrots and parsnips ensuring they are submerged in the liquid and continue to SLOW COOK for a further 2 hours.

HACKDONALD'S CHICKEN BURGER

Prep Time – 3m	Cook Time – 20m	Serves – 2

Difficulty: Easy
Ninja® functions: AIR FRY
Freezable: No

INGREDIENTS

Shop bought frozen chicken fillets in either a crumb or batter coating (pack of 4)
Brioche buns (pack of 4)
8 to 12 lettuce leaves (shredded)
2 to 4 tbsp of mayonnaise

Tips/Variations: If making 2 burgers, you may cook frozen chips at the same time in the AIR FRYING basket. If using fries style chips, they may be added after 5 mins of the chicken fillets going in. If thicker chips, they may need to go in earlier as they will require a longer cooking time.

DIRECTIONS

1. Place the air fry basket into your machine, select the AIR FRY function and set the temperature to 170 degrees and time to 3 mins and start – this is to preheat the machine. On some models, once this is complete, an ADD FOOD notification will appear.
2. Arrange the chicken fillets into the basket and set the time for 15 mins (still at 170 degrees) and leave to cook, flipping the fillets halfway. Note: you may need to adjust the cook time dependent on the size of the fillets that are being used so keep a check and alter as required.
3. Place the brioche buns into the basket and air fry with the chicken fillets for a further 1 min at 170 degrees.
4. Assemble the chicken, lettuce, mayonnaise and brioche buns into burgers and serve.

SPICY DONER KEBAB

Prep Time – 10m	Cook Time – 30m	Serves – One Complete Recipe	Gluten free✓

Difficulty: Easy
Ninja® functions: BAKE, AIR FRY
Freezable: Yes

INGREDIENTS

Any shop bought Doner Kebab seasoning of
your choice GF ** Use GF doner kebab mix
400g lamb mince (20% fat content)
1 tsp ground coriander leaf
1 tsp dried chives
1 tsp dried mint
1 tsp dried chilli flakes (optional)

Tips/Variations: If you do not have a blender, the ingredients can be kneaded together by hand. The meat can be prepared and left refrigerated overnight.

GF ** - Can be adapted to Gluten Free by
swapping the highlighted ingredients.

DIRECTIONS

1. Break up the lamb mince and place in a blender. Add in the seasoning mix and dried herbs. Blitz the ingredients together until a paste like consistency is achieved.
2. Form the meat into a giant sausage shape and wrap in cling film and place in the fridge for a good few hours to allow the flavours to infuse the meat.
3. Remove the meat from the fridge, one hour before cooking and remove the cling film.
4. Select the BAKE function on the machine and set the temp to 160 degrees. On some models the ADD FOOD notification will appear. Once ready, place the meat directly onto the grill plate in an ovenproof tin, or the air frying basket and BAKE for 25 mins.
5. Remove the meat from the machine and leave to go completely cold.
6. Once cold, slice the meat to preferred size and thickness. If the middle of the kebab appears like it isn't cooked, this will be completed at Step 7.
7. Before serving heat the sliced meat by placing it in a baking tin lined with foil and heat up using AIR FRY at 160 degrees for 4m. Adjust the time if required depending on thickness of the meat slices.
8. Serve in pittas with salad and garlic sauce.

PUB STYLE WAGYU BURGER AND CHUNKY CHIPS

Prep Time – 5 m	Cook Time – 17m	Serves – 2	Gluten free✓⬜

Difficulty: Easy
Ninja® functions: AIR FRY
Freezable: No

INGREDIENTS

2 wagyu burgers (shop bought, chilled) GF **
Use GF burgers
2 brioche buns GF ** Use GF buns
2 slices of sliced burger cheese
1 small red onion (peeled and thinly sliced)
Frozen chunky chips (to feed 2)
Burger sauce (optional)

Tips/Variations: None

GF ** - Can be adapted to Gluten Free by
swapping the highlighted ingredients.

DIRECTIONS

1. Select the AIR FRY function on your machine and set to 170 degrees for 15m.
2. Add the Wagyu burgers and frozen chunky chips to the air fry basket and cook together, flipping the burgers halfway and moving the chips around periodically.
3. Add the brioche buns to the basket and cook with the Wagyu burgers and chips at 170 degrees for a further 2 mins.
4. Assemble the burgers into the brioche buns, with the sliced burger cheese, sliced onions and burger sauce (optional) and serve with the chunky chips.

INTERNATIONAL

DISHES

CALZONE

Prep Time – 15m	Cook Time – 40m	Serves - 4

Difficulty: Easy/Medium
Ninja® functions: AIR FRY
Freezable: Yes

INGREDIENTS

2 pre-packed pizza base pastry halved
For the Tomato Sauce
250g passata
2 tbsp tomato paste
1 tsp minced garlic
1 tsp basil
1 tsp oregano
1 tbsp honey
For the filling/topping
250g mozzarella
6 sliced mushrooms
½ red onion sliced thinly
1 bell pepper sliced thinly
130g sliced chorizo
A few slices of pre sliced pepperoni
Pinch of basil to top

Tips/Variations: Change any of the fillings to suite you. Make it your own calzone.

DIRECTIONS

1. Add the tomato sauce ingredients to a bowl and mix.
2. Take out half a sheet of Pizza Dough, leaving it on the parchment sheet it came on.
3. Add some of the tomato sauce mix to the pizza sheet, but leave the edges free, keep some sauce for the top too.
4. Add all your chosen sliced fillings in layers to one side of the halved pizza base, then top with some Mozzarella, keeping some for the top when folded.
5. Fold and roll the edges inward together to seal it (like how a Cornish pasty is folded).
6. Lift the calzone into the air frying basket on the parchment paper and cook on AIR FRY 180 degrees for 5m, then turn over the calzone over for a further 5m on the same settings, using the parchment to help you do this.
7. Add the reserve tomato sauce and mozzarella to the top, with a sprinkle of basil and cook for a further 3 to 4m until all the cheese has melted.

LASAGNE

Prep Time – 20m	Cook Time – 35/40m	Serves – 4/6	Gluten free✓☐

Difficulty: Medium
Ninja® functions: PRESSURE COOK, SAUTE, AIR FRY
Freezable: Yes

INGREDIENTS

750g lean minced beef
1 garlic clove crushed
1 tsp oregano
1 tsp salt
½ tsp ground black pepper
1 tbsp sugar
1 onion diced
1 can chopped tomatoes
1 beef stock cube in 300ml of water GF ** Use GF cubes
1 tbsp tomato paste
150g cheddar cheese to top
Lasagne sheets GF ** Use GF sheets
For the Béchamel Sauce
50g butter
50g plain Flour GF ** Use GF Flour
450ml milk
Pinch of salt and pepper

Tips/Variations: If you don't want the Béchamel sauce, you can just buy a jar of white sauce or alternatively, cream cheese works so well and is my preferred flavour. Serve with salad.

GF ** Can be adapted to Gluten Free by swapping the highlighted ingredients.

DIRECTIONS

1. Add the minced beef, garlic, oregano, salt, pepper, sugar and onion to the main pot on SAUTE mode, MD heat (No. 3) until the mince has browned off.
2. Add the chopped tomato, stock and tomato paste to the pot and stir in. Let it heat through, then turn off. Set aside and clean the pot for the béchamel sauce. (Next step).
3. On the SAUTE function, LO/MD heat (No. 2), melt the butter, add the flour and stir into a paste. Gradually add the milk slowly, whist stirring, until you have a nice thick sauce. Keep adding until it's all poured in then add the salt and pepper. Clean the pot ready to assemble.
4. (In a round, deep cake tin) layer the minced meat mix, then lasagne sheets, then the white sauce. Do this until your mixture is used, normally 3 layers in total.
5. Fill the main pot with water to the 2 cups mark.
6. Add a low rack, place the tin onto it and PRESSURE COOK on HI heat for 30m, NATURAL RELEASE. Add the cheese and AIR FRY at 200 degrees for 8 to 10m.

MAC AND CHEESE

Prep Time – 5m	Cook Time – 20m	Serves – 2 to 3

Difficulty: Easy
Ninja® functions: PC, AIR FRY, MINI CHOPPER
for breadcrumbs, or you can use a grater.
Freezable: Yes

INGREDIENTS

300g macaroni
½ pint of milk
200g cheddar cheese grated
50g parmesan cheese grated
Pinch of salt
1 slice of bread made into breadcrumbs to top
Dried chives to top

Tips/Variations: You could also add diced
bacon to this. It can be used as a smaller side
dish or as a main. It goes well with fish. Also,
you can add a chicken stock to it when
PRESSURE COOKING for extra flavour.

DIRECTIONS

1. Fill the pot to just above 2 cups mark with water and add the pasta.
2. Set to PRESSURE COOK on HI for 5m, QUICK RELEASE. Once completed, empty any excess water out.
3. Add the milk, salt and 150g of the cheddar cheese and the parmesan to the pot with the pasta still inside. Retain 50g of cheddar cheese for the top later.
4. On SAUTE, MD heat (No. 3), let the cheese melt and milk heat through, it should start to thicken, then turn off the machine.
5. Add the reserve cheddar cheese to the top of the macaroni, followed by the breadcrumbs
6. Set to AIR FRY at 200 degrees for around 8m, or until the cheese is melted and the crumbs are crispy. Sprinkle the dried chives and serve.

CHICKEN FRITTERS

Prep Time – 15m	Cook Time – 20m	Serves – 2 (6 patties)	Gluten Free✓

Difficulty: Medium
Ninja® functions: DUAL MAX CRISP OR AIR FRY
Freezable: No

INGREDIENTS

1 frozen chicken breast
1 tsp dill
1/3 tsp pepper
1 egg
½ cup plain flour GF ** Use GF Flour
½ cup mozzarella grated cheese
2 tbsp mayonnaise
1 tsp MSG (optional)
Oil for spraying

Tips/Variations: You can serve with Fries, salad or in a roll with mayonnaise and lettuce.

GF **Can be adapted to Gluten Free by swapping the highlighted ingredients.

DIRECTIONS

1. Grate the frozen chicken into a bowl.
2. Add the dill, pepper, egg, flour, mozzarella, mayonnaise and MSG (if using). Mix all the ingredients together.
3. Line the stir-frying basket with foil and spray with a little oil.
4. Take around 3 tbsp of your chicken mixture and flatten into a burger shape on the foil.
5. MAX CRISP or AIR FRY at 200 degrees for 10m, turning halfway.

DEHYDRATED PORK

Prep Time – 5m	Cook Time – 3hrs	Serves - 2	Gluten Free✓

Difficulty: Easy
Ninja® functions: DEHYDRATE, AIR FRY
Freezable: Yes – ensure it is piping hot when reheated

INGREDIENTS

1kg pork joint
1 tbsp oil
Pinch of salt

Tips/Variations: This dish is also nice with herbs added to the oil to infuse the flavours. Fresh or dried both work well.

DIRECTIONS

1. Rub the oil all over the pork joint.
2. Add a sprinkle of salt
3. Place the joint in the machine in the air frying basket.
4. DEHYDRATE for 3 hours.
5. Switch to MAX CRISP or AIR FRY at 200 degrees for 12m

BREADED SALMON WITH DAUPHINOISE

Prep Time – 15m	Cook Time – 35/40m	Serves - 2	Gluten Free✓⬚

Difficulty: Medium
Ninja® functions: SAUTE or PC, BAKE, AIR FRY
Freezable: No

INGREDIENTS

4 white potatoes
1 garlic clove
1 tbsp olive oil
25g breadcrumbs GF ** Use GF breadcrumbs
2 salmon fillets
150g crème fraiche
1 stock pot GF ** Use GF stock pot
50g parmesan cheese
Pinch of salt
Pinch of pepper

Tips/Variations: This can be served with any vegetables and you can use light crème fraiche for a lower calorie version.

GF ** - Can be adapted to Gluten Free by swapping the highlighted ingredients for a gluten free version

DIRECTIONS

1. Peel and slice the potatoes into approx. 1cm slices, PRESSURE COOK on HI for 2m, QUICK RELEASE. Keep aside 75ml of the water (alternatively you could cook on SAUTE mode, MD heat, in water, boil until soft, approx. 8m. The potatoes need to be 'just covered').
2. In a bowl, grate half the garlic, add to the breadcrumbs with the oil and salt then mix.
3. Lay the salmon skin side down onto greaseproof paper, season with a pinch of salt and pepper.
4. Spread 1 tsp of the crème fraiche onto each of the fillets and add the breadcrumb mix to it, pressing down to make sure they stick.
5. Mix the remaining crème fraiche, grated garlic, vegetable stock, half the parmesan cheese, a pinch of salt and pepper and add this to the reserved potato water. Mixing it to make a smooth creamy sauce.
6. Preheat the dual drawer, or any other machine with the BAKE function at 180 degrees. You can lay straight in the drawer with the plate taken out or use a deep baking tray/cake tin.
7. Layer the potatoes, top with the sauce and BAKE for 15m at 180 degrees until starting to brown, then AIR FRY for 5 more minutes. The fish can be added after 10m on the same settings or if using the dual the other tray can be used 160 10m.
8. Serve with your choice of vegetables.

BREADED CHICKEN BREASTS WITH CHEESY MASH

Prep Time – 15m	Cook Time – 30m	Serves - 2	Gluten Free✓

Difficulty: Medium
Ninja® functions: Dual or AIR FRY
Freezable: Yes

INGREDIENTS

A handful of plain flour GF ** Use GF Flour
4 tbsp of milk
Panko breadcrumbs GF ** Use GF Bread
2 chicken breasts
2 tbsp olive oil
Sprinkle of salt and pepper
2 medium potatoes
Dash of milk, pinch of salt
Handful of grated cheese to top

Tips/Variations: Very tasty dish, nice with a glass of white wine.

GF ** - Can be adapted to Gluten Free by swapping the highlighted ingredients

DIRECTIONS

1. Peel and chop the potato in quarters and place in the air frying basket.
2. Fill the main pot up to the 2 cups mark with water, then PRESSURE COOK on HI for 4m, QUICK RELEASE. Empty out the water. In a bowl mash the potatoes with a little butter, salt and milk. Set aside.
3. Fill the main pot with water to the 2 cups mark, PRESSURE COOK the broccoli on HI for 1m, QUICK RELEASE. Set aside
4. Add the breadcrumbs to a bowl and mix with the olive oil to coat. This gives a lovely golden colour when cooked and helps keeps the breadcrumbs in place.
5. Spread the breadcrumbs out on a plate. The flour on another plate and the milk in a bowl.
6. Season the chicken breasts with a generous amount of salt and pepper. Roll in the flour until coated, tapping off any excess.
7. Dip the chicken breasts into the milk, then into the breadcrumbs, pressing firmly to coat all over. Do this on both sides.
8. Use a cutter to shape the mash and add grated cheese to the top.
9. Place the chicken in one side of the dual at 180 degrees for 25m on AIR FRY. And the mash and broccoli in the other side on parchment paper at 160 degrees on reheat 8m – press sync. Alternatively, if you don't have the dual, start cooking your chicken on the above function/time, then add the mash and broccoli when there's 7m left. Turn the chicken halfway. Serve and enjoy!

LIVER, SAUSAGE AND BACON CASSEROLE

Prep Time – 15m	Cook Time – 25m	Serves - 4

Difficulty: Medium
Ninja® functions: SAUTE, PRESSURE COOK
Freezable: Yes

INGREDIENTS

100g cubed liver
2 sausages
3 slices of bacon chopped
100g mushrooms chopped
1 large onion chopped
300g new potatoes
4 carrots peeled and chopped
400ml water
1 vegetable stock pot
2 beef stock cubes
1 tsp all-purpose seasoning
1 tsp Worcester sauce
1 tsp soy sauce (optional)
1 tsp brown sauce (optional)
Flour for coating liver
Handful of frozen peas
2 tbsp cornflour add to water and stir
A little oil

Tips/Variations: This works with most vegetables.

DIRECTIONS

1. Spray the main pot with oil, turn on SAUTE, MD heat (No. 3)
2. Coat the liver with flour, then fry in the pot with the bacon and sausage until browned.
3. Turn SAUTE setting down to LO/MD (No. 2). Add the mushrooms and onion and SAUTE for a further 2m.
4. Add the seasoning, stock and sauces.
5. In a jug, add 400ml of boiling water, add the vegetable stock, stir so it's all mixed in, especially at the very bottom and add to the casserole.
6. Add the potatoes and carrots and PRESSURE COOK on HI for 5m, NATURAL RELEASE.
7. Add the peas, then add the cornflour and stir to thicken.

MONGOLIAN BEEF WITH RICE

Prep Time – 10m	Cook Time – 25m or SC 2 -3 hours	Serves - 2

Difficulty: Medium
Ninja® functions: SAUTE, PRESSURE COOK or SLOW COOK
Freezable: Yes

INGREDIENTS

500g diced beef
1 tsp diced garlic or one clove crushed
1 onion diced
8 cup mushrooms chopped
3 tbsp sugar
3 tbsp light Soy
3 tbsp dark soy
2 tbsp plain flour
200ml water
1 tbsp oil
2 spring onions sliced to top
For the rice:
150g long grain white rice
350ml of cold water
1 tsp oil

Tips/Variations: This dish is also really nice with sesame seeds sprinkled over the top.

DIRECTIONS

1. On SAUTE, MD heat (No .3), add the oil to the main pot, brown off the diced beef, diced onions, garlic and mushrooms. Turn off the machine.
2. Add the flour and stir to coat all the ingredients.
3. Add the sugar, light soy, dark soy and the water and stir until it is all mixed together. Remove from the pot and place into a deep clean cake tin. Clean the pot and add 350ml of cold water to the bottom, place the Mongolian beef (in the cake tin) on the low rack and PRESSURE COOK on HI for 15m NATURAL RELEASE. Set aside the beef dish but keep warm. Empty out the water.
4. Add the rice and water with a tsp of oil to the main pot, PRESSURE COOK on HI for 3m, QUICK RELEASE.
5. Serve the rice and beef in a bowl and top with the spring onions.

PRAWN CURRY WITH COURGETTI SPAGHETTI

Prep Time – 10m	Cook Time – 15m	Serves - 2	Gluten Free✓

Difficulty: Medium
Ninja® functions: STEAM and SAUTE
Freezable: No

INGREDIENTS

1 small pack of medium sized prawns
(defrosted if frozen)
1 brown onion sliced
1 handful of fresh small/medium cauliflower
florets
1 tbsp garlic and ginger paste
1 tsp ground coriander
1 tsp cumin seeds
1 tsp ground turmeric
½ tsp lazy chilli or dried flakes
½ tsp black mustard seeds
½ tsp salt
½ can 400ml coconut milk
1 tbsp tomato paste
1 courgette sliced using a julienne peeler,
(courgetti spaghetti style)
1 tbsp oil
Parsley or chilli flakes to sprinkle on top.

Tips/Variations: This is also nice with peas and springe onions; you can leave out the courgette part and serve with rice or even in a toasted wrap.

I use a glass lid when steaming so you can lift and check throughout the process.

DIRECTIONS

1. Fill the main pot with water up to the two cups mark.
2. Add the fresh cauliflower florets and STEAM for 2 to 3m or until al dente or softer if you prefer. Set aside. Empty the water out.
3. Add the oil to the main pot on SAUTE, MD heat (No. 3)
4. Add the onions, cumin seeds, coriander, garlic and ginger paste, turmeric, chilli, mustard seeds and salt. Cook off the onions until their soft and the seeds are popping.
5. Add the coconut milk and tomato paste.
6. Stir it all together, then add the courgette, prawns and cauliflower until the prawns are all hot and cooked through. Serve, topped with some parsley.

SALMON AND WHITE WINE PASTA

Prep Time – 15m	Cook Time – 15m	Serves – 2 to 3

Difficulty: Medium
Ninja® functions: PRESSURE COOK, SAUTE
Freezable: No

INGREDIENTS

250ml of white wine
300g pasta spirals
300ml single cream
213g can of red salmon, de boned and
removed from can. Retain the juice
2 tsp paprika
2 chopped spring onions
150g of fresh prawns
2 garlic cloves
1 tbsp Italian mixed herbs
1 tsp black cracked pepper
Pinch of salt to taste
1 tbsp oil

Tips/Variations: You can use fresh salmon if you prefer, however the juices in the can are used and do give the dish that lovely flavour. Nice served with a glass of white wine.

DIRECTIONS

1. Fill the main pot to just over the 2 cups mark with water and add the pasta.
2. PRESSURE COOK on HI for 4m, QUICK RELEASE, empty the water out and set the pasta aside.
3. On SAUTE mode, MD heat (No.3) add the oil, salmon and the juices from the can, then the paprika, spring onion, prawns, garlic, mixed herbs, pepper, salt and wine. Stir continuously and heat through making sure the prawns are fully cooked. Adjust heat accordingly.
4. Add the pasta back in with the cream and let it heat through before serving.

TANGY BEEF AND TOMATO

Prep Time – 10m	Cook Time – 20m	Serves – 2

Difficulty: Medium
Ninja® functions: SAUTE
Freezable: Yes

INGREDIENTS

225g beef sliced thinly
2 chopped tomatoes
1 Small onion thinly sliced
2 tbsp vegetable oil
2 tbsp corn flour to a little water mix
240ml water
Pinch of salt
2 tbsp light soy sauce
½ tsp dark soy sauce
1 beef stock cube
1 tbsp sugar
1 tsp garlic puree
2 tbsp tomato ketchup

Tips/Variations: This is delicious served with some mini roasted potatoes or mashed potato.

DIRECTIONS

1. SAUTE, HI heat (no.5), add the oil and heat until hot. Add the beef and stir to brown off.
2. Turn down to LO/MD heat (No.2) and add the onion and cook until soft, stir.
3. Add the tomatoes, salt, ketchup, stock cube, both soy sauces, sugar, water and stir until the ingredients are cooked and it is all mixed together.
4. Add the mixed cornflour and water mix and stir to thicken.
5. Once it is all cooked and heated through, serve.

SLOW COOKED LAMB CHUMP IN GRAVY WITH CARROT AND ONION

Prep Time – 10m	Cook Time – 4 hrs	Serves – 2/4	Gluten Free✓⬚

Difficulty: Easy/Medium
Ninja® functions: SAUTE, SLOW COOK
Freezable: Yes

INGREDIENTS

2 lamb chump steaks
4 lamb stock cubes GF ** Use GF stock cubes
4 carrots peeled and ends chopped off
1 onion diced
2 sprigs of fresh rosemary
750ml water, boiled
4 tbsp plain flour GF ** Use GF flour
1 tbsp oil
Salt and pepper
1 tbsp mint sauce.

Tips/Variations: You can also add some chopped baby potatoes and peas for a more complete meal. This one makes the carrots and potatoes taste amazing!

GF ** - Can be adapted to Gluten Free by swapping the highlighted ingredients

DIRECTIONS

1. Brush the lamb chumps with a little oil and season with the salt and pepper, top with rosemary sprigs.
2. On SAUTE, HI heat (No. 5), place the chump steaks in the pot and brown all the sides of the meat to seal the flavours in.
3. Turn the pot down to MD heat (No. 3), add diced onion and stir until the onions are browned off then add the peeled whole carrots.
4. Add the flour and crumbled stock cubes to a jar with a pinch of salt and pepper, pour in some of the water, adding a little at a time whilst stirring, add a little more and keep doing this until it is all-mixed in. (The flour will thicken it).
5. Add the mint sauce and stir.
6. Pour the liquid mixture into the pot, whilst stirring and SLOW COOK on HI heat for 4 hours. Serve.

FAJITA SPICED CHICKEN, RICE AND BROCOLLI

Prep Time – 10/15m	Cook Time – 20m	Serves – 2/3	Gluten Free✓☐

Difficulty: Medium
Ninja® functions: STEAM MEALS
Freezable: No

INGREDIENTS

650g skinless, boneless chicken thighs
½ red pepper chopped
½ yellow pepper chopped
½ green pepper chopped
1 red onion diced
1 red chilli chopped
1 green chilli chopped
Fajita spice mix GF ** Use GF spice mix
Handful of tender stem broccoli per person
210g basmati Rice
500ml chicken stock GF ** Use GF stock
2 spring onions chopped to garnish
Pomegranate seeds to garnish

Tips/Variations: Garnish with any topping of your choice and you can also swap out the vegetables for your preference.

GF ** - Can be adapted to Gluten Free by swapping the highlighted ingredients

DIRECTIONS

1. Marinade the chicken in the spice mix and set aside.
2. Chop all the vegetables roughly into 1 cm cubes.
3. In the main pot, add 210g of basmati rice, the chopped vegetables and 500ml of chicken stock.
4. Add in the double rack, loosely wrap the broccoli up in foil and place on the bottom rack.
5. Insert the top rack and arrange the chicken onto it.
6. Close the SMARTLID, set the valve to VENT and slide the slider across to the middle section, select STEAM MEALS at 190 degrees for 9m.

BURRITOS WITH SECRET VEGETABLES (OPTIONAL)

Prep Time – 15m	Cook Time – 20m	Serves - 2	Gluten Free✔

Difficulty: Medium
Ninja® functions: SAUTE, AIR FRY
Freezable: Yes

INGREDIENTS

For the Filling:
250g lean minced beef
1 onion diced small
2 tbsp tomato paste
1 pack taco mix GF ** Check contents
½ can chopped tomatoes
2 beef stock cubes GF ** Use GF stock cubes
1 tbsp honey
1 tsp each of cumin, coriander and paprika
150ml water
3 wraps GF ** Use GF wraps
Pinch of salt to taste
Secret Veg:
Huge handful of spinach, kale and mushrooms
chopped finely
For the topping:
½ can chopped tomatoes
½ tsp garlic crushed and ½ tsp basil
1 tbsp tomato ketchup
1 tsp honey
Handful grated cheddar cheese + chives to top

Tips/Variations: You can of course leave out the secret veg, but honestly you don't know they're there, they are just like herbs. This is good for those who struggle with veg

GF ** - Can be adapted to Gluten Free by swapping the highlighted ingredients.

DIRECTIONS

1. Add the minced beef to the main pot on SAUTE, MD heat (No. 3). Start to brown off, then add the onions, mushrooms, spinach and kale and stir until cooked through.
2. Add the tomato paste, taco mix, chopped tomatoes, stock cubes, honey, cumin, coriander, paprika, water and salt. Bring to heat so it just starts to bubble, then turn off the machine.
3. Separately, blend the ½ can chopped tomatoes, then add the garlic, basil, ketchup and honey. Set aside.
4. Spoon the filling into the 3 wraps, folding the ends in, then rolling and arrange in an ovenproof dish. Pour on the tomato topping, add the cheese and chives and AIR FRY at 200 degrees for 8/10m. Serve.

PORK FILLET WRAP

Prep Time – 5m	Cook Time – 30m	Serves – 2	Gluten Free✔🔲

Difficulty: Easy
Ninja® functions: ROAST
Freezable: No

INGREDIENTS

1 pork fillet
16 streaky bacon rashers, unsmoked
4 pork sausage GF** Use GF sausage meat

Tips/Variations: Nice with wedges or roast potatoes and vegetables topped with lashings of gravy.

GF ** - Can be adapted to Gluten Free by swapping the highlighted ingredients.

DIRECTIONS

1. Roll some parchment paper out and lay the streaky bacon onto it, side by side and slightly overlapping.
2. Remove the sausage meat from the skins and press onto the bacon rashers.
3. Lay the pork fillet on the bacon in the opposite direction of the bacon rashers.
4. Using the parchment paper to help, roll up the fillet in the bacon and sausage. Like a sausage roll.
5. Discard the parchment paper and wrap the pork fillet in foil.
6. On the ROAST setting at 190 degrees, cook for 30m, remove the foil and cook for a further 10m, or until crispy.

MINTED LAMB BALLS AND FETA OMELETTE

Prep Time – 5m	Cook Time – 15m	Serves - 1	Gluten Free✓☐

Difficulty: Easy
Ninja® functions: MAX CRISP
Freezable: Yes

INGREDIENTS

1 minted lamb burger GF** Use GF Burger
½ red onion
1 red chilli
3 eggs
Handful of feta cheese

Tips/Variations: This dish is lovely topped with chilli sauce and minted yoghurt sauce.

GF ** - Can be adapted to Gluten Free by swapping the highlighted ingredients

DIRECTIONS

1. Pull apart the burger and roll into little balls.
2. Remove the crisp plate from the drawer. Set the dual max to MAX CRISP 15m and add in the lamb balls and cook for 5m.
3. Add the onion and chillies and cook for a further 1m.
4. Beat the eggs, then pour in and cook for around 1.5 m or until it has started to form a crust on top.
5. Top with the feta cheese and cook for a further 3m, or until it's done to your liking.
6. Slide it out of the machine and enjoy.

DEHYDRATED BEEF

Prep Time – 5m	Cook Time – 6hrs 34m	Serves – 6/8	Gluten Free✓☐

Difficulty: Easy
Ninja® functions: DEHYDRATE, AIR FRY
Freezable: Yes

INGREDIENTS

Beef joint 1.2-1.6kg weight

Tips/Variations: This is delicious served as part of a ROAST dinner, very tender.

DIRECTIONS

1. Place the beef joint into the air frying basket.
2. Set the machine to DEHYDRATE for 6.5 hours.
3. Once complete. switch to AIR FRY at 200 degrees and cook for 4m (rare), 6m (medium, rare), 8m (medium).
4. Cover with foil and leave to rest for 1 hour.
5. Carve and serve.

SAUSAGE STEAK PIE

Prep Time – 10m	Cook Time – 1 hr 10m	Serves - 4

Difficulty: Easy/Medium
Ninja® functions: SAUTE, PRESSURE COOK, BAKE
Freezable: No

INGREDIENTS

4 beef sausages
450g stewing steak
1 brown onion diced
2 beef stock cubes
1 vegetable stock pot
½ pint boiled water
Pinch of salt and pepper
60g plain Flour
I puff pastry sheet or a frozen block if preferred.
1 beaten egg to glaze
Dash of oil

Tips/Variations: This is best served with peas and chips and a little more gravy over the top.

DIRECTIONS

1. Put the flour in a bag with the salt, peppers and beef. Shake well to ensure the beef is thoroughly coated.
2. Add a dash of oil in the main pot on SAUTE, MD heat (No. 3) to fry off the beef until its browned (this may be done in two batches if it's easier). Take out and set aside.
3. On SAUTE, HI heat fry off the sausages until browned, then chop up using scissors. Add the onion and fry off until softened. Press pause.
4. In a jug, add the vegetable stock pot and stock cubes to the boiling water until dissolved. Pour slowly into the meat, stirring as you pour to ensure nothing is stuck to the bottom.
5. PRESSURE COOK on HI for 30m and NATURAL RELEASE. If the gravy requires thickening, add some gravy granules or cornflour.
6. Add the meat mixture to an ovenproof dish, cover with the pastry, slicing off any overhang with a knife. Brush the pastry with the beaten egg.
7. BAKE at 200 degrees for 30m. Enjoy!

SAGANAKI

Prep Time – 5m	Cook Time – 10m	Serves - 2	Gluten Free✓🗹

Difficulty: Easy
Ninja® functions: AIR FRY
Freezable: No

INGREDIENTS

225g halloumi cheese cut horizontal through the middle
1 beaten egg
Honey and sesame seeds to serve

Tips/Variations: For a different texture and flavour, you can also roll the cheese in semolina before frying and then finish with dried oregano and black pepper.

DIRECTIONS

1. Preheat the machine on AIR FRY at 180 degrees for 2m.
2. Dip the sliced cheese into the beaten egg mix so that it is fully covered.
3. AIR FRY for 8 to 10m or until golden brown.
4. Remove and spoon over some honey and then top with some sesame seeds.
5. Serve with pita bread, tzatziki, olives and tahini.

BULGOGI FISH

Prep Time – 12m	Cook Time – 15m	Serves - 2

Difficulty: Easy/Medium
Ninja® functions: AIR FRY
Freezable: No

INGREDIENTS

2 boneless haddock fillets (280g)
16 salted crackers crumbed
½ lemon Juiced
1 tsp bulgogi (medium heat BBQ sauce)
50g melted butter
Pinch of salt and pepper
2 tbsp of white wine

Tips/Variations: Delicious with fries and mushy peas.

DIRECTIONS

1. In the main pot on SAUTE, LO/MD heat (No. 2) melt the butter and add the Bulgogi sauce and the juice of the lemon into it. Stir. Set aside.
2. If you have the 3/1 or the MINI CHOPPER, you can whizz the crackers down in a few seconds. Alternatively, place in a bag and bash on a chopping board with a roller.
3. Place half of them into a baking dish.
4. Pat the fish dry and add a pinch of salt and pepper to both sides.
5. Lay the fish on the biscuit crumbs, add the melted butter mix over the top.
6. Add the rest of the crumbs to the top of the fish.
7. Add the white wine around the fish.
8. AIR FRY at 200 degrees for 15m.

CHICKEN AND CHORIZO TRAY BAKE

Prep Time – 10m	Cook Time – 20m	Serves - 2	Gluten Free✓

Difficulty: Easy
Ninja® functions: ROAST 10/1 oven (other
Ninja® machines can also be used)
Freezable: No

INGREDIENTS

2 spanish chorizo sausages (sliced)
2 chicken breasts, (diced)
1 red onion (sliced)
1 red pepper (sliced)
1 yellow pepper (sliced)
1 BBQ fajita seasoning packet GF ** Use GF
packet
1 tbsp oil
Spinach to serve
Caesar dressing GF ** Use GF dressing

**Tips/Variations: Delicious with Caesar
dressing drizzled all over it. Also nice served
with rice and topped with parmesan.**

GF ** - Can be adapted to Gluten Free by
swapping the highlighted ingredients

DIRECTIONS

1. Add the chorizo, chicken, onion, red and yellow pepper to a large bowl and drizzle on the oil and sprinkle in the fajita seasoning mix. Stir the ingredients together to coat the chicken.
2. Using a baking tray, spread out your food equally, place the baking tray into the oven and on the ROAST setting at 200 degrees, cook for 20m. Turn the tray bake a couple of times to ensure it is cooked/charred equally all over. (If you're using another machine, you can add the food to the air frying basket, with parchment laid at the bottom to prevent sticking, this may take less time to cook, so please keep a close check. You will still need to turn the food).
3. Serve on a bed of spinach with Caesar dressing drizzled over the top.

CHEESY CRISPY CHICKEN WITH SALAD

Prep Time – 10m	Cook Time – 20m	Serves - 1

Difficulty: Easy
Ninja® functions: AIR FRY, MINI CHOPPER
used (you can use any BLENDER)
Freezable: No

INGREDIENTS

1 chicken breast
1 soft brown roll GF ** Use GF bread roll
40g cheddar cheese chopped into 6 pieces
Pinch of salt
3 tbsp plain flour GF ** Use GF flour
1 egg (whisked)
Salad of your choice

Tips/Variations: For the sweetcorn, add to a ramekin, in water and AF for 7m stirring halfway. This also works with baked beans minus the water.

GF ** - Can be adapted to Gluten Free by swapping the highlighted ingredients

DIRECTIONS

1. Place the brown roll into the MINI CHOPPER with the cheese chunks/pieces and salt. Whizz down until the bread is all crumbed with the cheese in tiny pieces too. (You can use the PROCESSOR or any BLENDER to do this). Pour onto a plate. Set aside
2. Slice the chicken almost in half to butterfly it.
3. Put the flour onto a separate plate and the whisked egg into a wide dish. (Big enough to lay your chicken in flat).
4. Dip the chicken into the flour, turn it and make sure it's coated all over, then dip into the egg mix, turning and again, make sure it coated all over. Repeat the same with the crumb mix. Place the chicken on parchment paper and tip any remaining crumb mix over it. Wrap in parchment paper, then clingfilm and place in the fridge for 30m.
5. Remove the cling film and open the parchment, it can be cooked on the parchment paper to save cleaning, but ensure it is tucked in securely and is not touching the fan.
6. AIR FRY at 200 degrees for 20/25m, turning halfway and then serve. (If serving with sweetcorn, add the sweetcorn in a ramekin, cover the corn with water and cook for the remaining 7m to finish both together). Serve with salad.

BASA AND VEGETABLE TRAY BAKE

Prep Time – 10m	Cook Time – 40m	Serves - 2	Gluten Free✓⬚

Difficulty: Medium
Ninja® functions: ROAST
Freezable: No

INGREDIENTS

1 lemon
250g cherry tomatoes
2 tsp mixed herb
3 to 4 stalks of dill and parsley
300g white potatoes
2 garlic cloves
2 Basa fillets (also works well with sea bass or cod)
2 vegetable stock cubes or vegetable stock pot GF ** Use GF stock
Olive oil
Salt and pepper to taste
Knob of butter to serve

Tips/Variations: Roasting the garlic in its skin gives it a lovely, sweet flavour. A great dish to impress

GF ** - Can be adapted to Gluten Free by swapping the highlighted ingredients

DIRECTIONS

1. Mix the vegetable stock with 75ml of hot water and stir in the mixed herbs. Set aside for later.
2. Chop the potatoes into bite size pieces (skin on or off as preferred).
3. Lightly crush the garlic cloves, leaving them in their skin.
4. Put the potatoes in a bowl and add a good glug of olive oil, season with salt and pepper, stir to make sure the potatoes are completely coated in oil.
5. Add the cherry tomatoes and tip into the main bowl.
6. Set to 180 degrees on the ROAST setting and cook for 15/20m. Cook until the potatoes are starting to soften. Stir, making sure not to squash the potatoes.
7. Pour over the stock and place the fish on top of the potatoes, cut 4 slices from the lemon, squeeze the remaining juice over the fish and place the slices on top of the fish.
8. Turn on ROAST at 160 degrees and cook for 10/15m – keep checking.
9. Serve the fish on top of the roasted vegetables with a little butter on the potatoes. Hand shred the dill and parsley and sprinkle over the top. Serve.

VEGETABLE AND BACON CRUSTLESS QUICHE

Prep Time – 10m	Cook Time – 35/40m	Serves – 4/6	Gluten Free - ✓

Difficulty: Easy/medium
Ninja® functions: SAUTE, AIR FRY
Freezable: Yes

INGREDIENTS

Handful of peas
Handful of sweetcorn
Handful of spinach chopped
1 diced red onion
4 bacon rashers chopped
1 large bell pepper chopped
30g feta cheese chopped into small pieces
6 eggs
1 tsp multigrain mustard
A dash of milk
Pinch of salt and pepper
Handful of mature cheddar cheese
1 tbsp oil

Tips/Variations: You can mix and match your own vegetables of choice or just use ham, mushrooms and onions. It works with lots of variations and if the meat its fresh it can be frozen and re-heated.

DIRECTIONS

1. On SAUTE, MD heat (No. 3) add the oil, peas, corn, onion, bacon and bell pepper until the vegetables and bacon are all cooked and softened, lastly add the spinach to wilt. Remove, set aside and clean the pot.
2. Add the eggs to a bowl and whisk up, add the milk, salt, pepper, mustard and feta cheese. Stir. Add the vegetables to the bowl and stir again.
3. Pour into a dish, mine was not particularly deep, around 1 ½ to 2 inches.
4. Add the cheddar cheese to the top.
5. AIR FRY for around 35 to 40m at 180 degrees, ensuring that the egg is cooked in the middle and at the bottom.

PERI PERI CHICKEN TRAY BAKE

Prep Time – 10m	Cook Time – 1hr	Serves – 2/3	Gluten Free - ✓☐

Difficulty: Medium
Ninja® functions: ROAST
Freezable: No

INGREDIENTS

2 x 25g pk medium peri peri rub spice mix
1 red pepper
1 green pepper
1 red onion chopped into large chunks
1 red chilli
1 green chilli
1 large, sweet potato
650g boneless skinless chicken thighs
Oil for spraying

Tips/Variations: You can use any of your preferred spice mixes.

DIRECTIONS

1. Marinade the chicken in one and a half packets of the spice mix. Ideally leave in the fridge all day (but not essential).
2. Thread the chicken onto skewers and place them in a large roasting tin. Give them a good spray of oil.
3. Set the machine to ROAST at 180 degrees for 1 hour. Once preheated, place the chicken in to cook.
4. Chop the peppers and sweet potato into 3-4cm chunks. Once the chicken has been in for 10m, place the sweet potatoes around the chicken. Sprinkle the rest of the spice mix over them and cook for 20m.
5. Add the peppers and onion. Give it a good mix about in the juices and leave it to cook for a further 15m.
6. Slice the chillies, sprinkle on top and cook for a further 15m. Check that the chicken if fully cooked right through and the juices run clear before serving.

CHICKEN GYROS AND CHIP WRAP

Prep Time – 10m	Cook Time – 25m	Serves – 2

Difficulty: Easy
Ninja® functions: ROAST, AIR FRY
Freezable: No

INGREDIENTS

8 mini chicken fillets
3 tbsp crème fraiche
1 tsp each of the following: chilli powder, ground coriander, ground cumin, dried parsley
½ tsp each of the following: ground paprika (sweet or hot), garlic powder, dried oregano, dried thyme, ground cinnamon, salt
½ a lemon (juice only)
Frozen French fries (according to personal requirements)
4 Greek flatbreads (the soft ones)
Garlic sauce
Tomato, cucumber and red onion salad (portion size subject to preference)

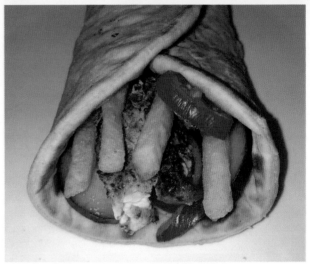

Tips/Variations: Greek yoghurt may be substituted for the crème fraiche.
These may be cooked directly in the main pot, the air frying basket or a foil lined tin in your machine.
The residual seasoning mix may be stored in an airtight container for future use.
The French Fries may be cooked ahead and then added in with the chicken at the AIR FRY stage to heat through.

DIRECTIONS

1. Mix together the dry ingredients to create the Gyros seasoning.
2. Mix together 2 tbsp of the seasoning with the crème fraiche and leave to one side.
3. Place the chicken fillets in a bowl and fork them all over and then squeeze the juice of the lemon over them.
4. Add the marinade to the chicken fillets and give them a stir to ensure they are completely coated and place in a sealed container and leave for a few hours in the fridge. Note: remove from fridge 1 hour before cooking.
5. Select the ROAST function on the machine and set to 170 degrees. Add the chicken (see Variations / Tips) and cook for 15 mins. Switch the function to AIR FRY and set to 190 degrees and cook for a further 3 mins.
6. Assemble the chicken with the French fries (see Variations / Tips), add garlic sauce and salad into the flatbreads and enjoy.

PILCHARD CURRY

Prep Time – 10m	Cook Time – 25m	Serves – 2	Gluten Free – ✓

Difficulty: Easy
Ninja® functions: SAUTE
Freezable: No

INGREDIENTS

1 small can of pilchards in tomato sauce
(155g)
2 tsp rapeseed oil
½ tsp cumin seeds
1 tsp garam masala
½ tsp chilli powder (optional)
1 pinch of salt
1 small onion (peeled and finely chopped)
1 birds eye chilli (chopped)
1 tbsp of tomato puree
Small handful of coriander (leaves only,
coarsely chopped)

Tips/Variations: Portion size may be increased by using a 400g can of pilchards in tomato sauce and doubling the ingredients except chilli which is dependent on personal spice and heat preferences.
Serve with chapattis, onion, chilli, salad and a heaped tbsp of natural yoghurt.

DIRECTIONS

1. Select the SEAR/SAUTE function and set to HI (No. 5) and press Start and add the oil.
2. Reduce heat to MD (No. 3) and add in the cumin seeds and toast them whilst stirring for 1 min to release the aroma.
3. Add in the onion, chilli, garam masala, chilli powder (if using) and salt and continue to SAUTE until the onions have softened with periodic stirring.
4. Add in the tomato puree and continue to stir for 1-2 mins.
5. Reduce the heat to LO/MD (No. 2) and add in the pilchards. Quarter fill the can with cold water and give it a swirl to get the tomato sauce from the sides of the can and add to the main pot.
6. Leave to simmer for about 5 to 7 mins and flip the pilchard fillets over halfway through to ensure the pilchards are heated through.
7. Garnish with chopped coriander.

SAGE AND CAYENNE PORK CHOPS WITH CARROTS

Prep Time – 10m	Cook Time – 12m	Serves – 2	Gluten Free - ✓🔲

Difficulty: Easy
Ninja® functions: STEAM MEALS
Freezable: No

INGREDIENTS

2 bone in pork chops (approx. 450g)
1 tsp all-purpose seasoning GF ** Check contents
1 tsp dried sage
½ tsp cayenne (adjust to suit personal heat preference)
Spray oil
2 large carrots (peeled and sliced into 1cm discs)
500ml cold water

Tips/Variations: You can use the juices from the chops to create a gravy.
If you have a foil tray that fits the chops, that may be used instead of creating one from regular foil.
Ninja® 'mash in a flash' is a great accompaniment to this meal.

GF ** - Can be adapted to Gluten Free by swapping the highlighted ingredients

DIRECTIONS

1. Mix together the all-purpose seasoning, dried sage and cayenne to create a rub.
2. Spray the pork chops with the oil and massage into the meat.
3. Coat the chops with the rub created in Step 1 and then set to one side for an hour.
4. Pour the cold water into the main pot.
5. Place a layer of foil on the low rack and arrange the carrot discs onto it.
6. Create a 'tray' using foil by folding up the edges so any meat juices remain contained that will fit on the top rack and place the pork chops into it and then place on top rack.
7. Place the assembled rack into the main pot.
8. Ensure that the rubber seal inside the lid is in place. Select the STEAM MEAL function, set the temp to 180 degrees and the time to 12 mins. Close the lid and set the valve to VENT and then press start.
9. Once the cooking process is complete, remove the rack and serve.

BOLOGNESE PASTA BAKE

Prep Time – 10m	Cook Time – 30m	Serves – 3 to 4

Difficulty: Medium
Ninja® functions: SAUTE, PRESSURE COOK, AIR FRY
Freezable: Yes

INGREDIENTS

500g minced beef
1 tbsp cooking oil
2 medium sized onions (peeled and finely chopped)
2 garlic cloves (minced)
1 tsp chilli powder (adjust to personal preference)
1 tsp of each - mixed herbs, salt, ground black pepper
2 tbsp tomato puree
1 jar of Bolognese sauce (500g)
Worcester Sauce (4-5 dashes)
Cold water (see Directions)
250g dried pasta shells
Grated cheddar
Chilli flakes (optional)

Tips/Variations: Sliced mushrooms may be added at Step 1 if you like mushrooms.
At Step 7, you can just leave the mixture in the main pot and top with cheese and chilli flakes (optional) and continue to cook.
'Cheatsway' Garlic Bread complements this meal perfectly!

DIRECTIONS

1. Select the SAUTE function at MD heat (No. 3) and press Start and add in the oil to heat through. Add in the onions and minced beef and stir until the meat has browned and the onions have softened.
2. Add in the garlic, mixed herbs, chilli powder, salt and pepper and stir. Then switch off the machine. Give the mixture a good stir to ensure nothing is stuck to the bottom of the main pot. This is sometimes referred to as de-glazing.
3. Add in the jar sauce, tip in the pasta, a few dashes of Worcester sauce, the tomato puree and enough cold water to come up to the top of the pasta. DO NOT STIR. Check the rubber seal is correctly in place on the SMART LID and that the valve is set to SEAL position.
4. Switch the machine back on and select the PRESSURE COOK function on HI heat for 6 mins followed by 2 mins NATURAL RELEASE. Note: if the machine has the DELAYED RELEASE function, this may be used instead.
5. Once the cooking is complete, the mixture may appear quite watery, in which case SAUTE may be used on HI (No. 5) to thicken up a little whilst stirring.
6. Transfer the mixture to an ovenproof tin and top with the grated cheese (a sprinkling of chilli flakes – optional) and wash and dry the main pot. Place the low rack into the main pot with the tin on it and select AIR FRY at 180 degrees and cook until the cheese is brown and bubbly to your liking.

'FLING IT IN AND WING IT' CHICKEN CURRY

Prep Time – 15m	Cook Time – 1½hrs	Serves – 2 to 3

Difficulty: Easy
Ninja® functions: SEAR / SAUTE
Freezable: Yes

INGREDIENTS

5 – 6 skinless, bone in chicken thighs
1.5 inch piece of fresh ginger
3 garlic cloves
2 finger chillies (adjust to suit personal heat preference)
4 sprigs of mint (leaves only)
2 small onions (bombay onions used, but not essential)
A handful of fresh coriander (leaves only)
1 tbsp vegetable oil
1 tsp each of: cumin seeds, garam masala, mango powder (amchoor – optional), dried fenugreek, ground turmeric, chilli powder, salt (to taste)
500ml boiled water
2 dsp low fat natural yoghurt

Tips/Variations: This is a good recipe to use up odds and ends in the fridge and does not require tomatoes as most curry bases often do. It is also made with ingredients that any curry lover may already have in the cupboard.
Best served with rice or chapattis.
Topped with fresh coriander.

DIRECTIONS

1. Place the onions, garlic, ginger, mint leaves, chillies and coriander leaves into a blender and blitz together until they appear finely chopped.
2. Select the SEAR/SAUTE function and set to HI (No. 5) and press Start.
3. Add the oil and allow a few minutes for it to heat up. Add the cumin seeds and SAUTE for a couple of minutes whilst stirring until they sizzle and brown.
4. Switch the heat setting to MD/HI (No. 4) and add in the chopped mixture from Step 1. Continue to SAUTE, whilst stirring until the onions have softened and the garlic and ginger have released their aromas.
5. Add in the spices - garam masala, chilli powder, mango powder, dried fenugreek, turmeric and salt and switch the heat setting to MD (No. 3) and continue to SAUTE, whilst stirring for 5-7 mins releasing the spice flavours. The ingredients will form a brown paste consistency.
6. Add in the chicken thighs and stir to coat in the spice paste and seal the meat all over.
7. Add in the boiled water and bring to boil (the heat setting may need to be increased for a few mins) and then switch the heat setting to LO/MD (No. 2) and cover with a glass lid and leave for 30 mins to simmer.
8. Stir in the yoghurt and cover with the glass lid and switch the heat setting to LO (No. 1) and leave for a further 30 mins to simmer. Garnish with chopped coriander leaves if using.

ONE POT CREAMY CHICKEN AND BACON PASTA

Prep Time – 5m	Cook Time – 30m	Serves - 2

Difficulty: Medium
Ninja® functions: AIR FRY, SAUTE, PRESSURE
COOK
Freezable: No

INGREDIENTS

250g pasta (linguini or spaghetti) broken in half.
½ onion diced
2 garlic cloves minced
1 chicken stock pot in 250ml of water.
Handful of grated cheese
250ml double cream
3 eggs
Handful of frozen peas
4 slices of smoked bacon
Handful of shredded pre-cooked chicken (I used 2
cups fulls but you can use what amount suits
you.)
Dash of oil and pinch of salt
Black pepper
Parmesan to top

Tips/Variations: Not for the faint hearted!

DIRECTIONS

7. AIR FRY the bacon in the crisper basket at 200 for 7m. Remove and set aside.
8. SAUTE the onion on MD heat (No. 3) until soft. Stir.
9. Add the peas and spaghetti to the pot and pour in the stock. Season with a little salt and a nice amount of black pepper. When you think there's enough black pepper, add more!
10. PRESSURE COOK on HI heat for 6m, QUICK RELEASE.
11. In a bowl, mix the cheddar, eggs and cream.
12. Turn pot to SAUTE, MD heat (No.3), break up the bacon and add it to the pot along with the shredded chicken.
13. Gently bring to heat, just to start the stock bubbling again, add the cheese and cream mix, stir all together. If it is too thick, you can always add a little water to it.
14. Serve in bowls and top with parmesan

VEGETARIAN SPECIALS

VEG AND SPELT CON CARNE

Prep Time – 15m	Cook Time – 20m	Serves - 2	Vegan✓◻

Difficulty: Medium
Ninja® functions: SAUTE
Freezable: Yes

INGREDIENTS

1 can of kidney beans
1 onion diced
1 red pepper diced
2 carrots diced very small
1 celery chopped
1 leek chopped very small
1 tin chopped tomatoes
1 can spelt
2 vegetable stock cubes
1 garlic glove
2 tbsp Worcester sauce (vegan)
3 tbsp tomato paste
2 tsp chilli (mild)
2 tsp each of paprika, ground cumin, ground coriander
1 tbsp natural raw sugar
Salt and pepper to taste.
1 tbsp Olive oil
200ml water

Tips/Variations: You can swap and change the vegetables around to suit. You can leave out the spelt and just serve with rice on the side if you prefer.

DIRECTIONS

1. Drain and wash the kidney beans and spelt thoroughly as per the instructions.
2. Add the oil to the main pot together with the diced onion, pepper, carrots, celery, leek and kidney beans, cook on SAUTE, MD heat (No. 3) until the vegetables are all soft, you may want to turn down and cook lower for longer.
3. Add the chopped tomatoes, garlic, spelt, stock cubes, Worcester sauce, tomato paste and cook for a few minutes, then add the rest of the ingredients.
4. Continue to SAUTE until it's all cooked through, stirring periodically until the vegetables are softened. Serve

VEGETABLE SOUP

Prep Time – 10m	Cook Time – 17m	Serves - 4	Vegan ✓	Gluten Free ✓

Difficulty: Easy
Ninja® functions: PC, BLENDER or use the Soupmaker
Freezable: Yes

INGREDIENTS

Handful fresh spinach, stems removed
Handful frozen peas
Handful fresh cauliflower florets
2 carrots chopped tiny
1 celery chopped
1 onion diced
1 green pepper chopped
2 vegetable stock cubes GF ** Use GF stock cubes
Salt and pepper to taste
Black pepper to top
750ml water

Tips/Variations: This is also very nice with kale, broccoli and asparagus. I like to keep it green!

GF ** - Can be adapted to Gluten Free by swapping the highlighted ingredients.

DIRECTIONS

1. Add the spinach, peas, cauliflower, carrots, celery, onion, pepper, salt, pepper and water to the main pot.
2. PRESSURE COOK on HI for 5m, then QUICK RELEASE.
3. Add the vegetable stock cubes.
4. Place the vegetable mixture in a BLENDER and blend until smooth. If you have the soupmaker this can be added and made in there on the SMOOTH SOUP setting.
5. Top with black pepper and serve with crusty bread.

STUFFED PEPPERS

Prep Time -10m	Cook Time – 15m	Serves - 2	Vegan ✓🗸	Gluten Free✓🗸

Difficulty: Medium
Ninja® functions: AIR FRY, SAUTE
Freezable: Yes

INGREDIENTS

2 red peppers
1 red onion diced
1 courgette diced
Handful of mushrooms diced
½ tsp salt
½ tsp smoked paprika
½ garlic clove crushed
½ tsp ground cumin
½ tsp coriander
½ tsp oregano
½ tsp chilli (mild)
1 tsp cracked black pepper
2 tsp vegetable oil
Handful of vegan grated cheese to top – Or if you're not vegan, normal cheddar

Tips/Variations: You can add different fillings. Rice works well added into the vegetables and equally you can remove anything you don't like, just pre-cook first.

DIRECTIONS

1. Put the oil in the main pot on SAUTE, MD heat (No. 3) and fry off the onion, courgette and mushrooms.
2. Add the salt, paprika, cumin, coriander, oregano and chilli. Set aside and clean the pot
3. Chop the top part of the red peppers off and take out the inside bits.
4. Spoon the filling inside
5. Top with the cheese and cracked black pepper.
6. Add to the basket and AIR FRY for 8m at 200 degrees. Serve.

RICE AND VEGETABLE RAINBOW

Prep Time – 10m	Cook Time – 20m	Serves - 2	Vegan ✓🌱

Difficulty: Easy
Ninja® functions: PRESSURE COOK, SAUTE
Freezable: Yes – make sure its piping hot
when reheated

INGREDIENTS

150g white long grain rice
350ml of cold water
1 tbsp oil
Handful of sweetcorn
Handful of peas
1 chopped red pepper
Pinch of chilli salt
3 tbsp light soy
3 tbsp dark soy

**Tips/Variations: You can swap the vegetables
for other preferred veg. Mushrooms work
well and onions too. Nice served with salad**

DIRECTIONS

1. Add the rice and water to the main pot.
2. PRESSURE COOK on HI for 3m, QUICK RELEASE. Take out and set aside.
3. Add the vegetables to the main pot with the oil and on SAUTE, MD heat (No. 3) cook and stir until it is cooked through.
4. Add the rice back in.
5. Add the soy sauces and chilli salt. Stir in and serve.

SPICY ROASTED CHICKPEAS

Prep Time – 5m	Cook Time – 20m	Serves - 4	Vegan✓	Gluten Free✓

Difficulty: Easy
Ninja® functions: FLAT PLATE
Freezable: No

INGREDIENTS

1 tin of chickpeas
2 tbsp garlic infused oil
2 tsp garlic granules
2 tsp chilli powder
1 ½ tsp onion powder
Salt and pepper

Tips/Variations: You can use a variation of different spices of your choosing.

DIRECTIONS

1. Drain and rinse chickpeas, then dry off gently with a clean tea towel and place them in a bowl.
2. Pour the oil over the chickpeas and add all the spices and a good grind of salt and pepper and give it a good mix.
3. Set the Max Pro GRILL (with flat plate in) to ROAST at 180 degrees for 20m. Once it is preheated, pour the chickpeas in and spread them out in a single layer and ROAST as above depending on the desired crispiness. Stir a couple of times whilst cooking.

JACKET POTATO

Prep Time – 2m	Cook Time – 40m	Serves - 1	Vegan✓	Gluten Free✓

Difficulty: Easy
Ninja® functions: AIR FRY
Freezable: Yes

INGREDIENTS

1 medium maris piper potato
Rapeseed oil (spray bottle)
Pinch of salt (fine sea salt)

Tips/Variations: For larger potatoes adjust the cooking time accordingly. You can cook as many potatoes the basket will hold at any one time.

DIRECTIONS

1. Fork the potato all over.
2. Spray with a little rapeseed oil and sprinkle of salt. Massage the oil and salt over the potato to coat. Place into the air frying basket of the machine.
3. Select the AIR FRY function and set to 180 degrees and cook the potato for 40m, turning periodically. Adjust timing to achieve the desired colour and crispiness to the potato skin.
4. Serve with your favourite filling

VEGETARIAN LASAGNE

Prep Time – 15m	Cook Time – 45m	Serves – 2/3	Vegetarian

Difficulty: Medium
Ninja® functions: SAUTE, PRESSURE COOK
Freezable: Yes

INGREDIENTS

A handful of peas
1 red pepper + green pepper
½ punnet chopped mushrooms
1 minced garlic glove
1 tsp oregano + 1 tsp Salt
½ tsp ground black pepper
1 tbsp natural raw sugar
1 diced onion
1 can chopped tomatoes
1 vegetable stock cube in 200ml of water
1 tbsp tomato paste
100g vegetarian cheddar cheese
Dried lasagne sheets
1 tub ricotta cheese
1 tbsp vegetable oil

Tips/Variations: This is best served with salad, garlic bread or fries.

DIRECTIONS

1. Add the oil to the main pot on SAUTE, MD heat (No. 3). Add the peppers, mushrooms, peas, onion and garlic, cook through. Adjust the heat as required.
2. Add the salt, pepper, sugar, chopped tomatoes, stock cube in 200ml of water and tomato paste and stir it all together.
3. In a cake tin, (mine was around 7"), place a layer of lasagne sheets, breaking them to make them fit. Then add a layer of ricotta (I added to the lasagne sheets before putting in the tin to make it easier to spread on). Next spoon on a layer of the vegetable mix, then repeat the layering of lasagne sheet, ricotta and vegetable mix until the mix is all used up.
4. The final layer should be lasagne, with ricotta and then finally the vegetarian cheddar cheese. Add foil to the top making sure it is secured tightly, to avoid it blowing up into the fan of the machine. In the main pot add just over the 2 cups mark with water and place your lasagne on the low rack to PRESSURE COOK on HI for 30m, NATURAL RELEASE 10m. Remove foil and AIR FRY at 200 degrees for 10m so the cheese is all bubbly and melted. Enjoy!

DEN'S MEXICAN BEAN AND RICE COMBO

Prep Time – 10m	Cook Time – 20m	Serves - 4	Vegan ✓🗆	Gluten Free✓🗆

Difficulty: Medium
Ninja® functions: SAUTE
Freezable: Yes, for the main bean dish

INGREDIENTS

1 tsp each of mild chilli, cumin, paprika
1 red pepper diced
1 can Mexican mixed bean – drained and rinsed.
1 carton of passata with garlic
150g sweetcorn
1 handful of chopped spinach
1 tbsp olive oil
1 heaped tsp natural raw sugar
1 vegetable stock Cube GF ** Use GF stock cubes
Pinch of salt
For the rice:
150g long grain rice + 350ml water
1 vegetable stock cube
For the guacamole:
1 avocado de-stoned and skin removed.
¼ red onion thinly diced
¼ wedge of lime (juice only)
½ garlic clove crushed and a pinch of salt

Tips/Variations:
To plate up:
Add the rice to one side of the dish, a little handful of spinach leaves next to that, then the Mexican beans. Top with a dollop of guacamole, vegan cream cheese and a sprinkle of chives.

GF ** - Can be adapted to Gluten Free by swapping the highlighted ingredients.

DIRECTIONS

1. **For the guacamole:** Add the avocado to a bowl and crush with a fork until smooth. Add the salt, diced onion and squeezed lime and garlic to it and stir to mix it all together (set aside until serving).
2. **For the rice:** Add the rice and water to the main pot, add the stock cube and PRESSURE COOK on HI for 3m, QUICK RELEASE. Cover with foil or parchment, then a tea towel to keep warm and set aside.
3. **For the Mexican bean:** Add to the main pot the pepper and onions with the oil. On SAUTE, MD heat (No. 3) cook until softened. Adjust the heat as necessary.
4. Add the passata, chilli, cumin, paprika, Mexican bean mix, sweetcorn, stock cube, salt, spinach and sugar. Stir all together. Bring to heat on MD SAUTE (No. 3) turn down to LO/MD (No.2) heat until everything is cooked through before serving.

PIZZA

Prep Time – 15m	Cook Time – 15m	Serves - 4	Vegan ✓☐

Difficulty: Medium/Advanced
Ninja® functions: SAUTE, BLEND (kneading function on the 3/1), AIR FRY
Freezable: No

INGREDIENTS

For the tomato sauce:
2 shallot onions chopped
1 garlic glove crushed
1 tin chopped tomatoes
1 tbsp tomato puree
1 tbsp natural raw sugar
1 tbsp white wine vinegar
For the pizza dough:
500g bread flour
1 tsp salt
300ml lukewarm water
1 packet of yeast
1 tsp sugar
Cheese to top

Tips/Variations:
Here are some suggested alternatives:
Onions
Tomatoes
Peppers
Sweetcorn
Vegan cheese

DIRECTIONS

1. On SAUTE, MD heat (No. 3). Add the shallots, garlic, chopped tomatoes, puree, sugar and wine vinegar. Bring to heat and cook through, then blend until smooth.
2. In a jug, add the lukewarm water (around 40 degrees), add the yeast and sugar. Leave for 5m until it froths.
3. In a bowl add the flour and salt, then add the yeast mix and stir in. Then use your hands to combine it together. Knead the dough on a flour base for 10/15m (or you can use the kneading blade in the 3/1 PROCESSOR)
4. Roll into 2 balls, add a little oil to a bowl, put the dough in the centre and add cling film to cover, leave to prove until it's doubled in size.
5. Take one ball out and flatten down, using fingers, push down and out to get the circle pizza shape (you can use a rolling pin too)
6. Add the tomato sauce and top with onion, mushroom tomato, or any of the above toppings finishing with your choice of cheese.
7. Preheat on AIR FRY for 5m at 210 degrees. Then cook the pizza for 10m 210 degrees. Enjoy!

CHEESE AND TOMATO MUSHROOM HEAVEN

Prep Time – 10m	Cook Time – 11m	Serves – Makes 8	Vegan✓	Gluten Free✓

Difficulty: Easy/Medium
Ninja® functions: GRILL, BLEND
Freezable: No

INGREDIENTS

1 shallot onion chopped
½ garlic glove crushed
½ tin chopped tomatoes
½ tbsp tomato puree
¼ tbsp natural raw sugar
½ tbsp white wine vinegar
8 portobello mushrooms
1 tbsp oil
Pinch of salt and pepper
Vegan cheese (or normal cheddar if preferred)

Tips/Variations: You can also change the toppings and serve on a bed of spinach or with a side of fries.

DIRECTIONS

1. Add to a bowl the chopped shallot, garlic clove, tinned tomatoes, tomato puree, sugar and white wine vinegar. Mix it all up together using the BLENDER. Set aside
2. De stem, oil and season the mushrooms with salt and pepper and place upside down on some foil or an ovenproof dish.
3. Cook on the GRILL setting, at the HIGHEST heat for 8m.
4. Turn the mushrooms over and fill with the tomato mix.
5. Top with Vegan cheese (or normal cheddar if preferred).
6. Cook on the GRILL setting HI heat until the cheese is all brown and bubbly. Serve

MEXICAN BEAN CASSEROLE WITH KALE MASH

Prep Time – 10m	Cook Time – 25/30m	Serves – 4	Vegan✓	Gluten Free✓

Difficulty: Easy/Medium
Ninja® functions: SAUTE, PRESSURE COOK, AIR FRY
Freezable: Yes

INGREDIENTS

1 can baked beans
1 can chopped tomatoes
1 can Mexican mixed beans
1 diced brown onion
2 vegetable stock cubes GF ** Use GF Stock
Pinch of salt
1 tbsp oil

For the mash:
4 white potatoes
¾ bag of kale, large stems removed, leaves only (chopped)
Pinch of salt

Tips/Variations: This is super healthy and tasty. Can be made in batches and frozen.

GF ** - Can be adapted to Gluten Free by swapping the highlighted ingredients.

DIRECTIONS

1. On SAUTE mode, MD heat (No.3) add the oil to the pot and then add the onion and cook until soft.
2. Drain and rinse the Mexican beans and add to the pot with the chopped tomatoes and the baked beans.
3. Give it a good stir and add the salt and vegetable stock cubes. Once it's all cooked through remove from the pot, clean and set aside.
4. Peel the potatoes and chop into 4 quarters. Fill the pot to the 2 cups mark with water, add the potato and the chopped kale. PRESSURE COOK for 4m, QUICK RELEASE
5. Retain the water but drain the potato and kale mix. In a bowl, add the potatoes, a large pinch of salt, then add a little of the water. Mash the potato mix, adding additional water to make it to the consistency of your liking.
6. Spoon the bean mix into an ovenproof dish or to the main pot and then spoon on the mash. Using a fork use a fork to create some lines in the mash and then AIR FRY at 200 degrees for 8m. Serve.

BLACK BEAN BURGER

Prep Time – 15m	Cook Time – 12m	Serves - 4	Vegan✓	Gluten Free✓

Difficulty: Medium
Ninja® functions: AIR FRY, (a burger press is handy)
Freezable: Yes

INGREDIENTS

2 cans of black beans, drain, rinse + pat dry
1 large, diced onion (finely chopped)
Pinch of salt and pepper
1 tsp cumin
1 tsp Lazy Garlic®
2 slices of brown bread, crumbed (vegan)
½ tbsp sriracha sauce (vegan) or dried chilli powder
1 tsp paprika
1 red bell pepper, diced small
4 burger rolls (vegan) GF ** Use GF rolls
4 lettuce leaves
4 tbsp tomato ketchup – sugar free (with extra for topping)
4 slices of red onion
1 slice of tomato
1 slice of vegan cheese

Tips/Variations: Drying the beans and crushing enough of them is important to help hold the mixture together better.

GF ** - Can be adapted to Gluten Free by swapping the highlighted ingredients.

DIRECTIONS

1. Drain, rinse and pat dry the black beans with kitchen towel. In a bowl, add the beans and mash, not completely, so some are still whole, but maybe ¾ mashed. Add the diced onion, pinch of salt and pepper, cumin, garlic, crumbed brown bread, 1 tbsp ketchup, sriracha sauce, paprika and diced bell pepper. Combine all the ingredients together with a wooden spoon.
2. Split the mixture into 6 to 8 portions. Roll each portion into a ball and form into a patty. It can be sticky, so a burger press makes this easier, or a little flour on your hands.
3. AIR FRY for 12m on 200 degrees, turning halfway.
4. Assemble the burger as follows: take the base of the roll and top with lettuce, burger, cheese slice, onion, tomato and then ketchup. Enjoy.

JUICING

GINGER AND TURMERIC HEALTH SHOT

Prep Time – 10m	Serves – 4 / 6	Vegan✓☐	Gluten Free✓☐

Difficulty: Easy
Ninja® functions: JUICER – No pulp
Freezable: Yes, this can be frozen as ice cubes too

INGREDIENTS

2 Inch piece of fresh ginger
2 Inch piece of fresh turmeric
2 red apples (cored)
4 lemons peeled
1 tsp honey
Pinch of black pepper

Tips/Variations: You can also freeze and have them as fresh orange or lemon, these are really refreshing in the summer. Also lovely as ice lollies.

DIRECTIONS

1. Peel the lemons.
2. Remove the core from the apples.
3. Put the honey and black pepper into the JUICING shoot that the fruit goes in as it carries it through and mixes it in.
4. Then put the turmeric through as the other fruits will help clean the colouring away.
5. Next the lemons and ginger then the apples.
6. Give it a little stir and serve in shot glasses.

THE ORANGE ONE

Prep Time – 15m	Serves - 4	Vegan✓🗹	Gluten Free✓🗹

Difficulty: Easy
Ninja® functions: JUICER – No pulp
Freezable: Yes

INGREDIENTS

2 bags of carrots
2 oranges
2 lemons
2-inch piece of fresh ginger fresh
2 mangoes peeled and de-stoned

Tips/Variations: Nice to freeze in an ice cube tray and serve added to fresh orange

DIRECTIONS

1. Chop the ends off the carrots and remove the peel from the mangoes, lemons and oranges.
2. Put half the carrots through the JUICING shoot.
3. Then the oranges, mango and lemons.
4. Add the ginger.
5. Then the rest of the carrots.
6. Serve.

LEMON AND GINGER ICE CUBE SHOTS

Prep Time – 10m	Serves – Ice Cube Portions	Vegan✓🗹	Gluten Free✓🗹

Difficulty: Easy
Ninja® functions: JUICER – No pulp
Freezable: Yes

INGREDIENTS

3 lemons
170g fresh ginger
2 apples
Fresh mint leaves

Tips/Variations: You can also serve in a glass of fresh lemonade or orange juice just to add a little summer zing to your drink.

DIRECTIONS

1. Chop the apples into quarters, peel the lemons and chop the ginger into small sections to fit into the JUICING feeder on the machine.
2. Now push through the fruit. Do a little of each at a time as it helps keep the barrel from getting clogged.
3. Now freeze overnight in ice cube trays.
4. Serve in a fresh glass of water with mint leaves, or put 2 to 3 ice cubes into a shot glass and leave to partly melt, then stir and knock back.

BANANA AND KIWI BLITZ

Prep Time – 5 m	Serves – 2	Vegan✓▢	Gluten Free ✔▢

Difficulty: Easy
Ninja® functions: SMOOTHIE
Freezable: No

INGREDIENTS

2 small bananas (peeled and cut into 3cm pieces)
4 kiwi fruits (peeled and quartered)
150ml chilled water
Mint leave to decorate

Tips/Variations: None

DIRECTIONS

1. Place all the ingredients into the jug of the SOUPMAKER and secure the LID.
2. Select the SMOOTHIE function to start the programme and let the machine do its magic.
3. Decorate as shown and serve.

CITRUS 'JUICEATHON'

Prep Time – 1	Serves – Multiple	Vegan✓🟦	Gluten Free ✓🟦

Difficulty: Easy
Ninja® functions: JUICER/ HI Pulp Filter
Freezable: Yes

INGREDIENTS

Orange Oomph - 8 large fruits (4 servings)
Groovy Grapefruit - 3 fruits (pink variety – 3 servings)
Marvellous Mandarin - 20 fruits (3 servings)

Tips/Variations: Once bottled, the juice may be frozen and then defrosted before being consumed. It is recommended that it is used within 3 months of being frozen to ensure its freshness and zinginess.
I keep and recycle plastic bottles, so these are from shop bought milkshakes and juice for example.
The juice may be topped up with chilled water (up to 100ml) to increase yield.
An internet search will provide ideas on how to use the pulp generated by the fruit to avoid food waste.

DIRECTIONS

1. Hand peel and prep the fruits.
2. Set up the Cold Press JUICER with HI Pulp Filter inserted.
3. Segment the fruits to a size to fit the feed tube on the JUICER and process through the machine.
4. Bottle as per photo.

MANGO MAGIC SMOOTHIE

Prep Time – 5 m	Serves – 2	Vegan✓	Gluten Free ✓

Difficulty: Easy
Ninja® functions: SMOOTHIE
Freezable: No

INGREDIENTS

1 mango (cubed)
1 banana (cut into pieces)
1 large orange (peeled, with pith removed
and split into segments)
250ml cold water

Tips/Variations: This is a good way to get some of your 5 a day the Ninja® way!
You could add two scoops of vanilla ice cream to create a milkshake style drink.
Indian mangoes are recommended when they are in season – this recipe used a Kesar mango which are usually available between May and August.

DIRECTIONS

1. Place all the ingredients into the jug of the SOUPMAKER and secure the LID.
2. Select the SMOOTHIE function to start the programme and let the machine do its magic.
3. Pour and serve.

WATERMELON REFRESHER

Prep Time – 10 m	Serves – 6	Vegan✓	Gluten Free – ✓

Difficulty: Easy
Ninja® functions: JUICER / MD Pulp Filter
Freezable: Yes

INGREDIENTS

1 medium sized ripe watermelon (cut into
10cm by 2cm fingers)

**Tips/Variations: The pulp could be used as a base
for a sorbet in the Ninja® Creami.**

DIRECTIONS

1. Prepare the fruit as described in ingredients.
2. Set up the Cold Press Juicer with Medium Pulp Filter inserted.
3. Feed the watermelon fingers through the tube on the juicer and decante into containers.
4. Chill in the fridge before serving or pour over ice for a glass of refreshing yumminess.

MANGO AND BLACKBERRY HEAVEN

Prep Time – 10 m	Serves – 2	Vegan✓🗹	Gluten Free – ✓🗹

Difficulty: Easy
Ninja® functions: JUICER / No pulp
Freezable: Yes

INGREDIENTS

2 mangoes
1 punnet of blackberries

Tips/Variations: This can be frozen as ice lollies for hot summer days.

DIRECTIONS

1. De stone and remove the skin from the mangoes.
2. Wash the blackberries.
3. Set up the Cold Press Juicer with No Pulp Filter inserted.
4. Feed the fruit through the tube and serve

SWEET TREATS &

ICE CREAM

VEGAN MANGO PASSION ICE CREAM

Prep Time – 5m	Freeze Time – 24hrs	Serves - 4	Vegan ✓	Gluten Free – ✓

Difficulty: Easy
Ninja® functions: SAUTE, ICE CREAM, BLEND
Freezable: Yes

INGREDIENTS

400g coconut milk
400ml plant-based milk GF ** Use GF
175g caster sugar
4 tbsp cornflour
1 tbsp vanilla bean paste
1 passion fruit
½ chopped mango chopped into small chunks
(Save the other half if you want to make
mango Sauce)

**Tips/Variations: You could add Vegan
chocolate drops and vegan topping instead of
the sauce**

GF ** - Can be adapted to Gluten Free by
swapping the highlighted ingredients.

DIRECTIONS

1. Mix the cornflour with a little milk to dissolve the flour. Dissolve the cornflour in a little of the plant-based milk.
2. Select SAUTE (No. 3) and pour in the coconut milk, vanilla bean paste, sugar, milk and cornflour into the main pot and bring to a simmer. Keep stirring until it thickens into a custard like consistency.
3. Pour into bowls and cover with cling film to prevent it forming a skin on top.
4. Allow to cool, then freeze for around 24 hours keeping the cling film on.
5. Remove cling film and put the ice cream into the Ninja CREAMI®, making a well in the centre.
6. Add the chopped mango and scraped out passion fruit to the well you have made
7. Press Mix in.
8. For the sauce, you can blitz down the other half of the mango using the BLENDER and pour over.

VEGAN SUMMER FRUIT ICE CREAM

Prep Time – 5M	Cook Time – 24hrs	Serves – 4	Vegan√⬜	Gluten Free – √⬜

Difficulty: Easy
Ninja® functions: SAUTE, ICE CREAM, BLEND
Freezable: Yes

INGREDIENTS

400g coconut milk
400 ml plant-based milk GF ** Use GF
175g caster sugar
4 tbsp cornflour
1 tbsp vanilla bean paste
Handful of mixed frozen berried

Tips/Variations: You could also make a berry juice for topping. Defrost the berries and use the BLENDER to blend it down to a juice and top your ice cream.

GF ** - Can be adapted to Gluten Free by swapping the highlighted ingredients.

DIRECTIONS

1. Mix the Cornflour with a little milk to dissolve the flour. Dissolve the cornflour in a little of the plant-based milk.
2. Select SAUTE (No. 3) and pour in the coconut milk, vanilla bean paste, sugar, milk and cornflour into the main pot then bring to a simmer. Keep stirring until it thickens into a custard like consistency.
3. Pour into bowls and cover with cling film to prevent it forming a skin on top.
4. Remove cling film and put the ice cream into the Ninja CREAMI®, making a well in the centre.
5. Add the frozen fruit to the well you have made.
6. Press Mix In.

JELLY ICE CREAM TREATS

Prep Time – 10m	Freeze Time – 24hrs	Serves - 4

Difficulty: Easy
Ninja® functions: ICE CREAM, MIX
Freezable: Yes

INGREDIENTS

1 cup whole milk
¾ cup double cream
2 tbsp caster sugar
2 tbsp Jelly powder – you can get various flavourings, these are lemon, blueberry and cherry

Tips/Variations: You can also add crushed Biscuits for a special treat and fruit segments.

DIRECTIONS

1. Place the above ingredients into the bowl and give it a mix together.
2. Cover with cling film and place in the freezer for 24hrs.
3. Take out, remove the cling film and press mix before serving.

LEMON DRIZZLE CAKE

Prep Time – 10m	Cook Time – 55m	Serves - 8

Difficulty: Medium
Ninja® functions: BAKE, BLEND (or use a handheld whisk)
Freezable: Yes

INGREDIENTS

170g self raising flour
170g margarine
170g caster sugar
3 medium sized eggs
2 lemons (juice and zest)
For the Drizzle
½ a cup of lemon juice
4 heaped tbsp of caster sugar

Equipment required

9" round deep cake tin
BBQ skewer to make holes in the cake.

Tips/Variations: You can put some butter icing in the middle or even ice the top, its lovely served when it's still warm with ice-cream.

DIRECTIONS

1. Blend together (using either the Ninja® or a hand whisk) the caster sugar and margarine until it goes whiter in colour.
2. Add the flour, eggs, lemon zest and juice then whisk together until all the ingredients are combined and again, the colour is lighter.
3. Line or grease a cake tin to fit the machine you are using and pour in the mixture. Levelling it out a little.
4. Add the low rack to the main pot and place the cake tin onto it.
5. Cook on BAKE setting at 140 degrees for 55m. No peaking! Remove from the machine.
6. On SAUTE, MD heat, add the sugar and lemon juice then stir until the sugar has melted.
7. Use the BBQ skewers to make holes in the cake, so when the drizzle is poured on, it will go right through the cake. Yummy!
8. Pour the drizzle over the cake. You can do this in the tin or place on a plate first then pour.

TEATIME GINGER BISCUITS

Prep Time – 20m	Cook Time – 15m	Serves – One complete recipe

Difficulty: Medium
Ninja® functions: SAUTE, BAKE, BLENDER
Freezable: No

INGREDIENTS

225g caster sugar
125g golden syrup
125g margarine
325g self-raising flour
3 tsp ground ginger
½ tsp ground cinnamon
1 tsp bicarbonate of soda
1 egg

Tips/Variations: Highly recommend dipped in a cuppa!

DIRECTIONS

1. Melt the sugar, syrup and margarine using the SAUTE setting on a very LO heat (No. 1)
2. In a bowl, add together the flour, cinnamon, ginger, bicarbonate of soda, eggs and lastly the melted mixture from step 1 and whisk together. (If you have a BLENDER, you can use this on MD speed setting)
3. Form the mixture into small balls by rolling in the palm of your hands, then flatten and place on some greaseproof paper, onto a baking tray.
4. Cook the ginger nuts using the BAKE setting at 160 degrees for around 15m, or until they are golden in colour and appear cracked.
5. Remove and cool on a rack before serving.

TRIPLE CHOCOLATE PANCAKES

Prep Time – 10/15m	Cook Time – 6m	Serves – Makes 8	Gluten Free✓🗌

Difficulty: Medium
Ninja® functions: FLAT PLATE
Freezable: Yes

INGREDIENTS

130g gluten free self-raising flour
1 tsp baking powder
1/2 tsp caster sugar
1 large egg
200ml whole milk
25g coco powder
50g white choc chips
50g milk choc chips
Pinch of salt
A little oil for the flat plate
1 tbsp golden syrup and a scoop of ice cream
to top

Tips/Variations: Other tasty toppings include strawberries, chocolate sauce and whipped cream.

DIRECTIONS

1. Add the flour, coco powder, baking powder, sugar and pinch of salt to a mixing bowl.
2. In a jug, beat together the egg and milk, then gradually whisk into the dry ingredients until a nice smooth batter is formed.
3. Add in the choc chips and stir.
4. Set the GRILL pro to FLAT PLATE at 200 degrees for 30m. Once preheated, give it a little spray with oil.
5. Add 2 ladles full of the mix (1 ladle per pancake, making two at a time).
6. Leaving the lid up, cook for roughly 2-3 minutes then flip over for 2 more minutes.
7. Repeat until the batter mix is all used up.

COCONUT CHOCOLATE DESSERT

Prep Time – 10m	Cook Time – 5m, sets in 2/3hrs	Serves - 2	Gluten Free✓▢

Difficulty: Medium
Ninja® functions: SAUTE
Freezable: Yes

INGREDIENTS

200ml coconut milk
100g chocolate chips GF ** Check contents
25g pistachio nuts
15g flaked almonds GF ** Check contents
1 dessert spoon of honey
Pinch of salt x 2
Dollop of clotted cream
3 strawberries, sliced

Tips/Variations: You may swap and change the toppings to suite your own preferences.

GF ** - Can be adapted to Gluten Free by swapping the highlighted ingredients.

DIRECTIONS

1. On SAUTE, HI heat (No. 5) bring the coconut milk to a boil and then simmer for 1m in the main pot.
2. Remove the main pot from the machine and add the chocolate chips and pinch of salt, allow it to stand for 1m, then stir together until the chocolate is melted.
3. Pour into a dessert dish and cover with cling film.
4. Refrigerate for 2/3 hours until its set.
5. Clean and dry the main pot.
6. Chop the pistachios and add them to the main pot on SAUTE mode, MD heat (No. 3). Dry fry them for around 3m, being careful to not burn them by constantly stirring.
7. Place the honey in a bowl and quickly tip the nuts in with a pinch of salt and mix.
8. Spoon the nuts onto the pudding with the flaked almonds, strawberries and clotted cream and serve. Better still, lock the doors and eat it all yourself!!

SPONGE CAKE

Prep Time – 5m	Cook Time – 55m	Serves - 8

Difficulty: Easy/Medium
Ninja® functions: STEAM BAKE
Freezable: No

INGREDIENTS

170g self raising flour
170g margarine
170g caster sugar
3 eggs
4 tbsp seedless strawberry jam
For the filling:
130g margarine
270g icing sugar

Tips/Variations: I sprinkled with dry icing sugar and topped with some chocolate buttons, but you can be creative with your top. Melted chocolate works and icing mixed with water drizzled. Also whipped fresh cream is nice with fresh strawberries.

DIRECTIONS

1. Add the flour, margarine, caster sugar and eggs to the BLENDER on MD spin if you have one, or hand whisk if you don't. Whisk until it changes to a lighter colour.
2. Fill the main pot with 3 cups of water.
3. Transfer the mixture to a large cake tin or mould and place directly in the AF basket in the 15/1. Or you can place the tin or mould on the low rack in the main pot.
4. STEAM BAKE for 55m at 160 degrees. No peaking at all! Or it will sink...
5. Lift out and leave until completely cooled, then slice in half.
6. Mix the margarine and icing sugar together to form a buttercream. Spread jam on to one half of the cake and the buttercream to the other and sandwich the two halves together.
7. Decorate with a dusting of icing sugar and / or your chosen toppings.

SCONES SERVED WITH CLOTTED CREAM AND JAM

Prep Time – 15m	Cook Time – 18m	Serves - 4

Difficulty: Easy/Medium
Ninja® functions: BAKE/ROAST
Freezable: Yes

INGREDIENTS

350g self raising flour
Pinch of salt
1 tsp baking powder
85g softened butter, cubed
3 tbsp caster sugar
175ml milk, plus a little extra to brush the scones before baking.
4 tbsp strawberry Jam
Tub of clotted cream

Tips/Variations: Sultanas may be added to the dough or for a more savoury taste, cheese and even a little chopped bacon works well.

DIRECTIONS

1. Place the flour, salt, baking powder and butter into a large bowl.
2. Rub between your fingers until it forms a crumbly mix.
3. Add the caster sugar and stir in.
4. Add the milk and stir in using a fork until combined. Using your hands, bring the mixture together gently to form a ball, but do not over work it.
5. Shake some flour onto a clean work surface and using an 10cm cutter, cut 4 large scones out of the mixture, this should be it all used up.
6. Add some parchment paper directly into the air frying basket of your machine.
7. Place the scones inside leaving as much space in between them as you can.
8. Brush the top with a little milk
9. Select the BAKE/ROAST setting at 190 and cook for 18m.
10. Serve with strawberry jam and clotted cream.

TRIPLE CHOCOLATE SCONES

Prep Time – 25m	Cook Time – 15m	Serves – 10/12	Gluten Free✓☒

Difficulty: Medium
Ninja® functions: (10/1 Oven) BAKE
Freezable: Yes

INGREDIENTS

315g gluten free self-rising flour
25g cocoa powder
1 tsp baking Powder
½ tsp xanthan gum
85g butter
4 tbsp caster sugar
175ml milk, plus extra for brushing the tops
before baking
70g milk chocolate chunks
50g white chocolate
2 ½ inch cookie cutter required
Clotted cream and chocolate spread to fill

Tips/Variations: These were filled with chocolate spread and clotted cream but can use any filling of your choice.

DIRECTIONS

1. Dice the butter into small cubes (the colder the butter the better)
2. Place the gluten free self-rising flour, cocoa powder, baking powder, xanthan gum and caster sugar into a bowl. Add in the butter cubes.
3. Rub together with your fingers until it forms a breadcrumb like texture.
4. Pour in the milk and using a metal spoon work it together until it starts to form a dough.
5. Flour a clean work surface and continue to work it a little more until it's all come together.
6. Flatten it out slightly with your hands until it's just over an inch in thickness.
7. Sprinkle some of the milk chocolate chunks all over the top of the dough and gently press in. Flip the dough over and do the same on the other side.
8. Use the cookie cutter to cut out the scones. Reform any offcuts to make more until the dough is used.
9. Place them on a baking tray lined with greaseproof paper and brush the tops with milk.
10. Preheat the oven and cook on BAKE setting at 190 degrees for 12 to 15m. Remove, add your melted white chocolate by drizzling over the top. (It can be melted in a microwave in short bursts)

CLASSIC DUAL VICTORIA SPONGE

Prep Time – 10m	Cook Time – 55m	Serves - 6

Difficulty: Easy/Medium
Ninja® functions: BAKE
Freezable: No

INGREDIENTS

250g caster sugar
250g softened butter
5 eggs (beaten)
250g self-raising flour
1.5 tsp baking powder
3 tbsp milk
For the filling:
150g softened butter
200g icing sugar
170g of good quality strawberry jam
Icing sugar and fresh strawberries to decorate

Tips/Variations: This is best served with your feet up and a cuppa next to you, whilst gazing out on a beautiful view. Or I guess you could also share it...

DIRECTIONS

1. This step will help you take the finished cake out of the drawer. Cut a strip of greaseproof paper (15 cm wide x 44 cm long – 17cm wide for the newer model).
2. Grease both ends and the bottom of the drawers. Lay the paper along the bottom and up both ends. Trim any overhang at the top.
3. Beat the caster sugar, butter, eggs, self-rising flour, baking powder and milk together until they form a smooth soft batter. (If you have the PROCESSOR, you can use this with the paddle attachment).
4. Divide the mixture between the drawers, smooth the surface. Set draw 1 to 150 degrees on the BAKE function, press match and start. BAKE for 45m, then turn up to 170 degrees for a further 10m keeping a check on it. (A skewer should come out clean and if you push the top with your finger, it should spring back up).
5. Leave to cool in the drawers for 5m, then lift out using the greaseproof paper tabs at each end and place on a cooling rack to cool completely.
6. To make the filling, beat the softened butter and sifted icing sugar until it's smooth and creamy. (Again, this can be done using the PROCESSOR, bowl and mixing blade attachment).
7. Spread the buttercream over the bottom of one of the sponges, top it with 170g of strawberry jam and sandwich the second sponge on top. You can get creative with your own toppings, but I put some more butter icing on mine with fresh strawberries. Enjoy!

BANOFEE PIE

Prep Time – 20m	Cook Time – 40m	Serves – 6/8

Difficulty: Easy/Medium
Ninja® functions: PRESSURE COOK, BAKE
Freezable: No

INGREDIENTS

397g condensed milk
250g Biscoff® biscuit crushed
120g butter unsalted and melted
2 bananas (sliced into 1 cm discs)
300g double cream
1 tsp vanilla extract
Dark chocolate shaving or cocoa powder to dust.

Tips/Variations: This is delicious as it is and needs no tips to make it better, enjoy!

DIRECTIONS

1. Place the low rack in the main pot and add the can of condensed milk (leaving the contents still inside and removing the can wrapping first). Fill with enough water to cover and immerse the tin.
2. PRESSURE COOK for 30m on HI, QUICK RELEASE. Empty pot.
3. Place the can of condensed milk in some cold water to cool, you can add ice to speed up the cooling process. (Use heat protection gloves for this step)
4. Crush the Biscoff® biscuits into small crumbs, add the melted butter and stir with a wooden spoon to coat the crumb. (This can be done in the main pot on SAUTE, LO/MD heat (No.2/3).
5. Add the biscuit mixture to an 8-inch pie/cake tin using a glass to push up the sides. BAKE for 8m on 160 degrees. Place in the fridge to cool.
6. Whip the cream and vanilla extract until peaks are formed.
7. Once the condensed milk has cooled, add it to the biscuit base, spreading it level.
8. Add the sliced bananas, then the cream. Top with chocolate shavings or cocoa powder.
9. Refrigerate for 30m. This will last up to 3 days in the fridge.

RICE PUDDING

Prep Time – 5m	Cook Time – 20m	Serves - 4	Gluten Free✓

Difficulty: Easy
Ninja® functions: PRESSURE COOK
Freezable: No

INGREDIENTS

100g pudding rice
700m milk (whole or semi skimmed)
50g sugar

Tips/Variations: A dollop of strawberry jam, honey, or a sprinkling of nutmeg is a great compliment to this dish.

DIRECTIONS

1. Rinse the rice in water ensuring all starch is removed.
2. Add the rice to the main pot, followed by the milk and sugar and give it a good stir.
3. PRESSURE COOK on HI for 15m, NATURAL RELEASE.
4. Serve.

CRÈME BRULEE

Prep Time – 10m	Cook Time – 30m	Serves - 4	Gluten Free✓

Difficulty: Medium
Ninja® functions: PRESSURE COOK, GRILL, SAUTE
Freezable: No

INGREDIENTS

360ml double cream
60g sugar + additional for topping
4 egg yolks
Pinch of salt
1 tsp vanilla essence

Tips/Variations: There are simply no variations to this, it's dreamy and creamy just as it is.

DIRECTIONS

1. In the main pot, on SAUTE mode, MD heat (No. 3) add the cream and heat until it is just starting to bubble, remove the pot and place on a heatproof mat.
2. In a separate bowl, beat the egg, sugar and salt together.
3. Pour a little of the hot cream into the mixture and stir. Continue to add and stir until it's all mixed together.
4. Pour into 4 ramekins/pots and cover with foil.
5. Add 2 cups of water to the main pot, place the low rack into the pot and arrange the ramekins/pots onto the shelf.
6. PRESSURE COOK on LO for 7m, then NATURAL RELEASE for 15m.
7. Remove ramekins/pots and cover with cling film, leave to cool, then refrigerate for 3 hours.
8. When ready to serve, remove cling film and cover the top with Sugar of your choice and with a blow gun, melt the sugar (alternatively you can GRILL on HI until the sugar has caramelized).

APPLE OAT CRUMBLE PUDDING

Prep Time – 15m	Cook Time – 35m	Serves - 4	Vegan√	Gluten Free√

Difficulty: Easy/Medium
Ninja® functions: BAKE
Freezable: No

INGREDIENTS

For the apple:
5 granny smiths apples peeled, cored and sliced
1 tbsp lemon juice
1 tbsp brown sugar
1 tsp cinnamon
For the oats:
300g oats GF ** Use GF oats
85g dairy free butter (room temp)
85g brown sugar

Tips/Variations: This is also delicious with raisins or sultanas, a dash of honey and served with ice cream as above.

GF ** - Can be adapted to Gluten Free by swapping the highlighted ingredients.

DIRECTIONS

1. In a bowl, completely coat the oats with the butter and sugar.
2. In a separate bowl, coat the apple in the lemon juice, then add the sugar and cinnamon, stir.
3. Place the apple mixture in an ovenproof dish/cake tin and cover with the oat mixture. Place on the low rack/trivet.
4. Cook on the BAKE function, at 160 degrees for 35m.
5. Serve.

BANANA ICE CREAM MIX

Prep Time – 40m	Serves – 1 Bowl	Vegan✓☑	Gluten Free✓☑

Difficulty: Easy
Ninja® functions: BLENDER, CREAMI
Freezable: Yes

INGREDIENTS

3 ripe bananas (skins removed)
¼ cup of frozen orange smoothie mix
½ cup frozen pomegranate
1 tbsp 100% Pure maple syrup

Tips/Variations: Great with a serving of strawberries or just on its own.

You can also add to ice cream moulds for those hot summer days, great for the kids too!

DIRECTIONS

1. Lay the banana in bags separately so they freeze individually for 3 to 4 hours.
2. Remove from freezer and pop into the BLENDER and pulse to start with, add the maple syrup then blitz.
3. Add the orange smoothie mix and pomegranate and blitz until all combined into ice.
4. Put into a bowl and freeze for 30m.
5. Select your favourite ice-cream programme on the Ninja CREAMI®. I used smoothie bowl.
6. There will be pips from the pomegranate in the mix.

JAM SPONGE CAKE

Prep Time – 5m	Cook Time – 55m	Serves - 8

Difficulty: Medium
Ninja® functions: STEAM BAKE, PROCESSOR
(or an electric whisk is the same)
Freezable: No

INGREDIENTS

170g self raising flour
170g caster sugar
170g margarine
3 large eggs
4 tbsp strawberry jam
175g icing sugar
1 tbsp water

Equipment required
Large cake tin 9"

**Tips/Variations: Sit down, relax and enjoy
with a cup of tea.**

DIRECTIONS

1. Add to the PROCESSOR bowl the margarine, sugar, flour and eggs, then whisk on MD speed until all the ingredients are combined for approximately 1 to 2m (add to a bowl and whisk if you don't have the PROCESSOR).
2. Fill the pot with water to the 2.5 cups mark and place the air frying basket into it.
3. Put the cake case into the air frying basket and pour the cake mixture into it.
4. STEAM BAKE at 160 for 55m.
5. Remove and set aside to cool.
6. Once cooled spread the jam directly on top of the cake.
7. In a jug, add a tbsp of water to the icing and stir until combined. It needs to have a runny consistency so that it may be drizzled over the cake as shown in the photo.
8. Pour over side to side, turn the cake and go side to side again to achieve a drizzled effect.

STRAWBERRY ICE CREAM

Prep Time – 15m	freeze Time – 24hrs	Serves - 4	Gluten Free✓

Difficulty: Easy/Medium
Ninja® functions: PROCESSOR/BLENDER, SAUTE
Freezable: Yes

INGREDIENTS

400g strawberries
600ml double cream
300ml whole milk
150g white caster sugar
5 egg yolks
2 tsp lemon juice
2 tsp vanilla extract,

Tips/Variations: Lovely served with fresh strawberries

DIRECTIONS

1. Place the strawberries in the PROCESSOR/BLENDER and whizz down to a puree, add the lemon juice and vanilla extract.
2. On SAUTE, MD heat (No. 3), warm the cream and milk up, just to when it starts steaming, then (Pause).
3. Whisk the sugar and eggs in a bowl until a pale-yellow colour is achieved (around 2 m). Strain with a sieve to remove any access egg white, then add to the cream and stir to mix it into a custard on a LO heat (SAUTE No. 2). It should coat the back of the spoon when done and should leave a channel when you run your finger through it.
4. Pour the mixture into a bowl to cool down for 10m and then chill for 1 hr in the fridge.
5. Stir the strawberry puree, lemon and vanilla through the cold custard. Add in additional vanilla extract or lemon juice to suit taste at this point.
6. Freeze for 24hours. (You can use the Ninja Creami® for the desired blend)
7. Keeps frozen up to 2 months.

YOGHURT

Prep Time – 2m	Cook Time – 9 to 12 hours	Serves – 4/6	Gluten Free✓

Difficulty: Easy
Ninja® functions: YOGHURT
Freezable: Yes

INGREDIENTS

110g natural yoghurt
1 litre semi skimmed milk

Equipment required
Muslin straining bag/cloth

**Tips/Variations: Scale up your ingredients for a larger batch.
Serve with vanilla flavourings, honey, seeds or fresh strawberries.**

DIRECTIONS

1. Ensure the main pot is very clean.
2. Tip the milk into the main pot, set to YOGHURT mode and press start. The milk will come up to just under boiling point and it will say cooling. It then drops the temperature to about 45 degrees (this takes hours, so you can cheat by taking out the pot and putting in in cold water and use a kitchen thermometer if you have one).
3. Stir in the starter (yoghurt) and switch the machine to fermentation (by pressing temp and turn the control clockwise while in yoghurt mode) Set for 9 hours.
4. After the 9 hours is up, your yoghurt is done.
5. To turn this into Greek style yoghurt, strain for 2 to 3 hours, depending on how thick you like it. The longer you leave it, the thicker it gets.
6. Also, if you make it too thick, you can spoon back in the whey that you have drained off and give it a stir.

TOASTER JAM SPONGE CAKE

Prep Time – 5m	Cook Time – 30m	Serves - 4

Difficulty: Easy
Ninja® functions: BAKE in the 3/1 toaster
Freezable: No

INGREDIENTS

113g self raising flour
113g margarine
113g caster sugar
2 eggs
150ml double cream
4 tbsp strawberry jam

Equipment required

2 4.7" cake tins lined
Piping bag

Tips/Variations: Lovely with a glass of lemonade in the sunshine or a cup of tea when it's raining.

DIRECTIONS

1. Line the cake tins
2. Place the flour, margarine, sugar and eggs then whisk together either with a handheld whisk or the Ninja® PROCESSOR, MD speed for 1 to 2m.
3. Split the mixture equally between both tins.
4. Remove the PANINI PRESS and place the tins on the main tray, select the BAKE function and cook for 30m on MD heat (175 degrees).
5. Check after 20m that it's not touching the GRILL top, rotate/twist the tins horizontally if necessary to ensure an evenly baked sponge.
6. Remove and leave to cool down.
7. Once cooled spread the jam on both sides (I turned mine upside down for the perfect levelled cake, cutting any uneven bits from the top first).
8. Whisk the double cream until its stiff and won't run out if tipped upside-down.
9. Pipe the cream onto the jam on both cakes and then sandwich together. I did the bottom too for extra decoration. Enjoy!

INDEX

- GF ** - Can be adapted to Gluten Free by swapping the highlighted ingredients.

- GF - Naturally Gluten free recipes do not require ingredients substitution as they are gluten free as listed

- VE – Suitable for Vegans

- V – Suitable for Vegetarians

Printed in Great Britain
by Amazon

12332103R00078